ARKANSAS TORNADOES:

The Natural State's Deadliest Twisters

ARKANSAS TORNADOES:

The Natural State's Deadliest Twisters

Marlene Bradford

Cover photo from NOAA Photo Library, NOAA Central Library;
OAR/ERL/National Severe Storms Laboratory (NSSL)

To my dear friend Wanda McCaslin Adams who provided encouragement and support to keep me writing

Contents

Contents

Acknowledgements

A special thanks belongs to many who helped in making this book a reality.

Librarians in many small towns throughout the state, especially those in Warren, Judsonia, and Jonesboro, helped me locate materials from their communities. David Ramsey and Bill Albright at the Cleburne County Historical Society in Heber Springs went out of their way to find information for me.

Wanda Carey sent me entire newspapers from several counties with accounts of the 2008 tornadoes. In addition, she and her husband John squired me around Little Rock and Heber Springs and provided me a place to lay my head at the end of the day.

Without the help of my husband Bill, who often had to pick up housekeeping and cooking duties so I could finish a chapter, the writing would have taken much longer.

Introduction

"Hurry up! Get to the cellar. There's a bad cloud coming." My mother-in-law, like generations of Arkansas women before her, did not have a television or radio to receive a warning, but she knew from the appearance of the clouds that a life-threatening tornado could appear at any moment. For most of the year the storm cellar served as storage for canned goods and extra potatoes and onions, but in the spring and early summer it took on a more serious role--saving lives. In spite of the presence of cellars in so many yards across the state, tornadoes have killed hundreds of Arkansans from the first recorded touchdown in Pulaski County in 1823 to the present.

Arkansas is in the center of tornado activity in the United States. To the west is the traditional Tornado Alley of the Great Plains, and to the southeast is the Gulf region which in the last few decades has become the new tornado hot spot, Dixie Alley. In spite of its relatively small geographic size and population, Arkansas ranks among the top five states in the number of tornadoes, deaths, deaths per million people, and killer tornadoes since 1880.

With few exceptions the deadliest tornadoes came with companions. Only two twisters in recorded Arkansas history that claimed more than 20 lives were stand-alone storms: Pine Bluff in 1947 and Green Forest in 1927. Determining which tornadoes to include in this book was a difficult task. I have chosen to focus on superlatives: the deadliest tornadoes and outbreaks both before and after 1953 (considered the beginning of the modern era because of the advent of tornado forecasting and warnings), the deadliest day, year, and decade, the longest tornado, and the largest number of tornadoes in one day. In addition, I have included a few tornadoes that do not earn a superlative but are historically important. The accounts encompass more than fifty counties and several hundred towns and communities these storms visited from 1898 through

2020. Many who read the book will be able to relate personally to at least one of the tornadoes, either through connection to the locality or acquaintance with someone who witnessed them. It is my hope, however, that those who read the accounts of the horrific death tolls and devastation these monsters of nature left behind will heed the safety measures necessary to survive if a tornado approaches their community.

Chapter 1

Tornado Characteristics

Cyclone, twister, whirlwind, tornado—the word varies in time and place—but all refer to one of nature's most destructive storms. Regardless of the name attached to the storm, it often leaves behind death and devastation.

Tornadoes are as unique as humans--no two are alike. A tornado usually appears as a white, gray, or black funnel-shaped cloud, but some tornadoes may resemble a wall of smoke rolling across the landscape. A tornado has a distinct life cycle. It is usually born as a thin funnel descending from the parent thunderstorm cloud. As it matures and expands, the rotating column of air picks up material in its path and acquires the color of the circulating debris. In its dying stage the funnel may appear as a long, thin rope. During all stages the tornado is capable of massive destruction. Most tornadoes last only a few minutes, but a few stay on the ground for up to two hours.

Some tornadoes have multiple vortices, two or more small funnel clouds orbiting a central point. The small vortices (often called suction vortices) of a multiple vortex tornado are generally responsible for the small but extreme paths of destruction. They can also explain why tornadoes supposedly "skip" houses—one house may sustain little damage while the one across the street may be destroyed.

Frequently a weather system produces numerous tornadoes in a short period of time. The definition of a tornado outbreak has varied over the decades. Dr. Greg Forbes generally defines an outbreak as "the group of tornadoes spawned by the same weather system, but that is still a little vague. I usually include in an outbreak all of the tornadoes in a contiguous-state region over a period in which there is no more than a six-hour tornado-free gap." The largest outbreak in the United States occurred on April 27-28, 2011, when 199 tornadoes killed 316 residents of five southern states. The deadliest Arkansas outbreak took 111 lives on March 21, 1952.

LOCATION

About one-half of the world's tornadoes develop within the United States where conditions for their formation are ideal: a moisture source to the south, a cold source to the north, mountain ranges to the west, deserts to the southwest, and an active jet stream. Historically, these meteorological conditions have converged most often from Texas northward through Nebraska, an area frequently called "Tornado Alley," but in recent decades a "Dixie Alley" has seemingly developed in the states of Arkansas, Mississippi, Alabama, and Tennessee, causing great death and destruction in the South Central and Southeastern United States. More than twenty other countries, including Canada, Argentina, Australia, France, England, Italy, Germany, India, China, Bangladesh, Japan, and South Africa have tornadoes.

The 2263 tornadoes recorded in Arkansas from 1950 through 2020 were not distributed evenly across the state. Pulaski County (97) and Scott County (8) were the extremes. The map of tornado touchdowns below shows the greatest number occurred in Pulaski, Lonoke, and White counties while many counties along the southern (Lafayette) and northwestern (Boone and Carroll) borders experienced very few twisters.

TIME

Tornadoes strike during every month of the year in the United States, but peak months vary by region. The prime season in the Southeast is March through May, while May and June are the most active months in the Midwest, the Northwest, and the southern Great Plains. The northern Great Plains, the Rocky

Mountain region, and New England experience the most tornadoes June through August, and the Gulf Coast states have a second tornado season in November. In Arkansas almost two-thirds of the twisters occur in the spring. April has the distinction of being the most active month while July is the least active. Although tornadoes may strike at any hour of the day, the peak hours in Arkansas are from 4 to 8 PM with the most occurring about 5 PM.

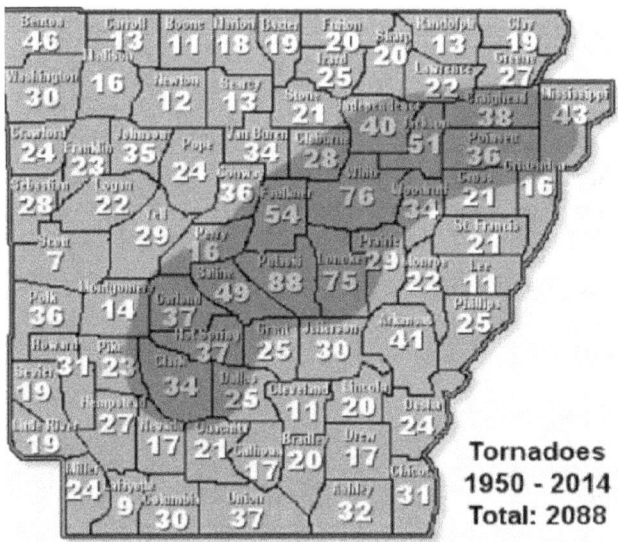

Arkansas Tornado Alley. NWS Little Rock.

WIND SPEED

Tornadoes are nature's most violent windstorm. Only a few hurricanes have achieved wind speeds of over 150 miles per hour, but tornadic winds quite commonly exceed that speed. Because tornadic winds destroy anemometers and the possibility of a tornado passing over such an instrument is remote, indirect methods are required to determine a twister's wind speed. In 1970 Dr. Theodore Fujita devised a method of estimating tornadic wind speeds based on the destruction the storm left behind. Since 1971 the National Weather Service has assigned, when possible, a Fujita or F-scale rating to every reported tornado. In addition, the National Severe Storms Forecast Center (now the Storm Prediction Center) used photographs and damage reports to retroactively rate all tornadoes since 1950. In 2007 the National Weather Service began using the Enhanced Fujita Scale to rate tornadoes. The new scale lowers the wind speeds in each category but still relies upon destruction of structures and vegetation. The Storm Prediction website lists the 59 tornadoes that have received the F5/EF5 rating during the period 1950-2014. Since 1950, the overwhelming majority of Arkansas tornadoes have been F0 or F1. Only one tornado in Arkansas history has achieved an F5/ EF5 rating, the April 10, 1929, storm that struck the Sneed community in Jackson County.

The Enhanced Fujita Tornado Scale

FUJITA SCALE			OPERATIONAL EF-SCALE	
F Number	Fastest ¼-mile (mph)	3 Second Gust (mph)	EF Number	3 Second Gust (mph)
0	40-72	45-78	0	65-85
1	73-112	79-117	1	86-110
2	113-157	118-161	2	111-135
3	158-207	162-209	3	136-165
4	208-260	210-261	4	166-200
5	261-318	262-317	5	Over 200

MOVEMENT

The average tornado moves across the landscape at speeds from thirty to fifty miles per hour, but a few twisters whirl along at speeds up to sixty miles per hour while others virtually stand still. Tornadoes can travel in any direction, but in the United States almost 80 percent of them move from southwest to northeast or west to east. Twisters do not always follow a straight line. In the dying stage many veer toward the north or south. Some follow a circular route; a few return along the path of destruction they have already left behind.

SIZE

The majority of tornadoes cut short, narrow paths across the land. The average path width is 128 yards, and the average path length is 4.4 miles. What may be the widest tornado ever recorded in the United States (2.6 miles) occurred near El Reno, Oklahoma on May 31, 2013. The longest tornado may have been the Tri-State Tornado of 1925 which traveled 219 miles across parts of Missouri, Illinois, and Indiana.

The widest Arkansas tornado, just over 1.6 miles in width, was the April 25, 2011 Pulaski/ Faulkner/White Counties storm. The longest recorded tornado path entirely within the state of Arkansas occurred on February 5, 2008. This single twister tracked 122 miles from Centerville (Logan County) to Highland (Sharp County).

SOUND

Tornadoes do not come quietly. Their noise is often heard several miles away. As the storm approaches, it usually emits a peculiar high-pitched whistling sound that rapidly changes to an intense roar. Eyewitnesses most often describe a tornado's sound as like a freight train or low-flying jet airplanes.

NUMBER

Tornado statistics may be misleading. Many that touch down at night or in remote areas go unreported. Studies have suggested that only one-third to one-half of the tornadoes in the United States are counted. Nineteenth-century severe weather enthusiasts compiled lists of tornadoes covering short periods of time, but the accuracy varied from person to person and from state to state. John Park Finley, the country's first tornado authority, counted thirty-four tornadoes that caused twenty-nine deaths and $535,000 worth of damage from 1840 to 1886 in Arkansas. The United States Weather Bureau began officially counting tornadoes in 1916, but it usually counted only tornadoes that caused deaths or substantial property damage; weak storms rarely appeared in the official data. To verify the effectiveness of its tornado watches, the Weather Bureau began a serious effort to count all tornadoes in 1953. The National Climatic Data Center (NCDC), the official U.S. government database for all weather events, lists 75,515 tornadoes in the United States from 1950 through 2020. *However, the NCDC counts tornadoes by county-segments; therefore, one tornado that crosses into three counties will be counted three times which leads to an inflated number of tornadoes.* The most tornadoes recorded for one year was 2066 for 2011 (remember that this is counted by county segments; the actual number of tornadoes is much lower). The least recorded was 201 in 1950.

Tom Grazulis, a tornado statistician who established an independent database, listed 755 significant tornadoes (those that caused a death or were rated F2 or greater) in Arkansas during the years 1880-1991. The NCDC recorded 2071 tornadoes from 1950 through 2015. During that period the highest number of tornadoes reported for one year was 140 in 1999, and the lowest was one in 1963. Regardless of which statistics one uses, Arkansas ranks in the top five states in the number of tornadoes, deaths, deaths per million people, and killer tornadoes.

DEATHS

Almost 15,000 Americans died in tornadoes during the twentieth century. The worst single year was 1925 with 794 fatalities; the lowest yearly death toll was fifteen in 1986. Tornado death statistics before the 1950s may be inaccurate though. In the nineteenth century blacks were commonly underreported as deaths. In addition, many died after the tornado from injuries the storms inflicted upon them, and there was no organization in charge of weather statistics until the mid-twentieth century. Although the numbers may not always be accurate, without doubt a tornado watch and warning system instituted in the 1950s combined with improved communications and tornado safety education has substantially decreased the loss of life from twisters in the United States.

The country's worst single tornado (although recent research revealed that this event may have been multiple tornadoes) occurred on March 18, 1925, when 695 died across Missouri, Illinois, and Indiana. A look at the list of the twenty deadliest tornadoes in the United States (see appendix A) reveals they occurred in numerous states and struck from March to June.

Arkansas has suffered a disproportionate number of tornado deaths. The state is the 27th largest in land area in the United States, yet it lost 1597 residents from 1880 through 2020, the fourth highest number in the country. The Natural State has the dubious distinction of leading the country in the number of deadly tornadoes per square mile. Tornado deaths since 1950 have not been evenly distributed across the state. Only fifty of the seventy-five counties experienced a tornado death, and a majority of those counties recorded fewer than five deaths. White County led in fatalities with sixty; the only other counties suffering more than twenty deaths are Craighead (37) and Woodruff (32). For a complete list of the number of tornadoes and deaths by county since 1950, see Appendix B.

Deadliest Individual Tornadoes in Arkansas History

RANK	PLACE	DATE	DEATHS
#1 (tie)	Fort Smith	January 11, 1898	55
#1 (tie)	Warren	January 3, 1949	55
#3	Rural areas	April 15, 1921	51
#4	Judsonia/Bald Knob	March 21, 1952	50
#5	Brinkley	March 8, 1909	49
#6	England/Cotton Plant	March 21, 1952	40
#7 (tie)	Pine Bluff	June 1, 1947	35
#7 (tie)	Jonesboro	May 15, 1968	35
#9	Berryville	October 29, 1942	29
#10	Center Point	April 16, 1939	27

Deadliest Tornado Outbreaks in Arkansas History

RANK	DATE	#OF DEATHS	HARDEST HIT AREA
#1	March 21, 1952	111	Judsonia
#2	June 5, 1916	75	Heber Springs
#3	March 8, 1909	67	Brinkley
#4 (tie)	November 25, 1926	58	Heber Springs
#4 (tie)	January 3, 1949	58	Warren
#6	April 10, 1929	55	Swifton/Sneed
#7	May 9, 1927	46	Strong
#8	March 1, 1997	25	Saline County

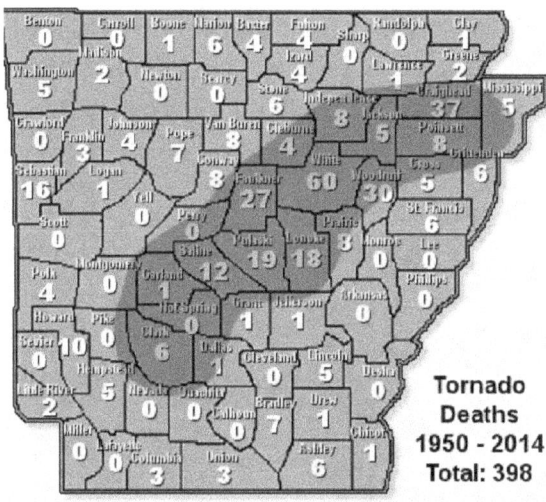

Deaths in Arkansas Tornado Alley. NWS Little Rock

WHY SO MANY DEATHS IN ARKANSAS?

1. Before 1953 the United States had no system of tornado watches and warnings.

2. Topography may play a role. The western half of the state is hilly, and residents cannot see a tornado approaching as readily as those in the Plains states can. Trees obscure the view in the heavily-forested southern counties. Hills also hinder television and radio signals.

3. Most homes did not have a television until the late 1950s, and television stations in the state were minimal. Today some sections

of the state rely upon television weather broadcasts from surrounding states which may not adequately warn the Arkansas segment of the viewing audience.

4. Arkansas is under the jurisdiction of National Weather Service offices in five states which might lead to miscommunication between the offices and the Arkansas television stations. Most of Arkansas receives its weather warnings from the Little Rock NWS Office, but counties near the state's borders are in the warning areas for Tulsa, Shreveport, Memphis, and Jackson.

National Weather Service offices that oversee Arkansas. NWS

5. Many storms in Arkansas occur outside the usual spring tornado season. The two deadliest tornadoes in Arkansas history (Ft. Smith and Warren) struck in January.

6. Walker Ashley, meteorologist at Northern Illinois University, suggests three other factors: mobile home density, the number of tornadoes that occur at night, and complacency or the idea that it can't happen here. He notes that "Oklahoma is known worldwide

for the frequency of its tornadoes. Yet the state has fewer fatalities than Arkansas, Alabama, and Mississippi."

ODDITIES

Tornadoes are capricious by nature. Virtually every twister leaves behind stories of strange occurrences such as food left untouched on the table when the entire house is gone. Many of these unusual happenings can be attributed to random chance. If enough houses are struck, the odds are in favor of a refrigerator being hurled into the top of a tree or the contents of a dresser drawer being rearranged. Some oddity reports are obviously false. No wind can defy the laws of nature by blowing a two-gallon jug inside a quart bottle without cracking either one or turning an iron teakettle inside out. Until recently, many of these unusual happenings added to the belief that tornadic winds far exceeded 300 to 400 miles per hour, but an extremely high wind speed is not needed to blow a pig into a tree top, pluck feathers from a bird, or carry a human several hundred feet.

TORNADO SAFETY TIPS

1. **Assume every tornado is a deadly one**. Avoid staying in its path, if possible. If it isn't possible to avoid the tornado, have a place to take shelter.
2. Learn the difference between a tornado **watch** (tornado **could happen** somewhere during the time of the watch) and a tornado **warning** (a tornado **has been sighted** in your area—take the necessary precautions to protect yourself and others). Whenever a watch is issued for your area, be sure you have a way to keep up with the weather. Phone apps from television stations and various weather entities are available which will notify you in case of a tornado warning in your area. Some cities such as where I live have a reverse 911 call service to notify residents, even in the middle of the night. If possible, have a weather alert radio,

especially if you live in a mobile home or in an area susceptible to night time tornadoes.

3. At home put as many walls between you and the outside as possible. This is usually a downstairs bathroom or closet, but be sure the room does not have a window or an outside wall. If your house has a basement, take shelter there. In a two-story home a good place is often a storage area under the stairs. I always told my students that if they had time to put on sturdy rubber-soled shoes (if your house is hit, there will be broken glass and maybe downed electric wires), to be sure they had their cell phone in their pocket, and to grab something such as a pillow, chair cushion, blanket, or even a bicycle or football helmet to cover their head. The old myth of opening windows should be ignored. Don't waste time—the first thing the winds will do is open them for you.

4. **Mobile homes are especially vulnerable to high winds**. Anyone who lives in a mobile home, whether it is tied down or not, needs to leave and seek shelter in a sturdy building. If your mobile home park has a community shelter, go there.

5. At school, follow the instructions of the principal or person in charge.

6. Ask if your workplace has a designated safe area. If not and you are in a multi-story building, the stairwell is a good place as are inside bathrooms, but stay away from windows and get downstairs as much as possible.

7. Many malls have designated tornado or safety shelter. Look for them if severe weather is a possibility on your shopping day.

8. In restaurants, grocery stores, or convenience stores walk-in coolers or refrigerators are the best places to go; bathrooms are also a possibility, but be sure they don't have windows.

9. **Cars are not a safe place to stay in a tornado**. If you are in a car and see a tornado approaching, leave your car and take shelter in a sturdy building. If you are out in the country and no building is available, get into a ditch or a culvert. Be sure to get away from your car. There are cases of people being killed by their car rolling on top of them. DO NOT GET UNDER A HIGHWAY BRIDGE OR OVERPASS—they act as wind tunnels. If you are traveling on the highway, be sure you know what county you are in should the

weather turn severe. Tornado warnings are usually issued by county.

10. If you find yourself in the open when a tornado is approaching, try to get to a building. If none is available, find a low place such as a ditch and get as flat to the ground as possible.

11. **No matter where you are, when a tornado watch is issued, think about where you would take shelter and, most importantly, KEEP INFORMED ABOUT THE WEATHER.**

Chapter 2

The Deadliest Day: March 21, 1952

"It was just flat and barren, everything blown away." One World War II Pacific campaign veteran said the area looked like Eniwetok, but the battleground was not the site of a conflict between opposing armies of men but of opposing forces of nature. On March 21, 1952, a cold front advancing eastward encountered warm, tropical air. The battlefield (or "squall line") lay 100 miles ahead of the front. As the approaching colder, denser air forced the warmer surface air aloft, storm clouds formed. Opposing winds swirled around each other, and cumulonimbus clouds pushed higher and higher into the atmosphere. From this dark rotating mass dangled at least 10 tornadoes. When the battle moved eastward into Tennessee and Mississippi, Arkansans totaled their casualties—111 dead and 787 injured.

The front page of the March 21 *Arkansas Democrat* displayed a short article entitled "Storms Due Tonight in S. Arkansas." The United States Weather Bureau in Washington, D.C., issued the following forecast at 11:55 A.M. (CST): "A few isolated tornadoes may occur late this afternoon and this evening in southern Arkansas, northern Louisiana, extreme southeastern Oklahoma, and the north half of eastern Texas." The Little Rock office said it was very unlikely that the severe thunderstorm activity would reach into the central Arkansas area, but the Little Rock vicinity could receive thundershowers. Tornado forecasts were extremely new. The Weather Bureau had issued its first official one only four days earlier, but no tornadoes formed within the designated area. The U.S. Air Force's Severe Weather Warning Center located in Oklahoma City also new to the tornado forecasting game, issued a tornado forecast (now known as a "watch") on the morning of March 21 for an area along and fifty miles north of a line from Greenville, Texas, to Monticello, Arkansas. Later that afternoon, the Air Force revised the forecast to include an area bounded by Walnut Ridge, Monticello, Texarkana, and Dyersburg (Tennessee), but the Weather Bureau did not revise its prediction. According to Joseph Galway, one of the Weather Bureau's first severe weather forecasters, the March 21 forecast was a success because four tornadoes (three in Arkansas) occurred within the designated area and time period.

Issuance of a tornado forecast is only the first step in saving lives. A watch means the meteorological conditions are favorable for storm formation, but there is no guarantee that tornadoes or even thunderstorms will appear. To adequately warn the public two additional factors are necessary—a tornado spotting network and an extensive communications system. Arkansas had neither in 1952. Arkansans in the path of the Friday evening tornadoes had little or no access to warnings. In 1952 Arkansas had no television stations, and according to the 1950 United States Census only 6,090 or 1.2 percent of the homes in the state had a television set. Over 10 percent of the homes did not have even a radio. To add to the problem, local radio stations signed off the air at sundown. As a result, few residents of the stricken towns knew a tornado was coming although the twisters had been marching eastward across the state during much of the afternoon and evening.

The first tornado to batter Arkansas on March 21 roared into Dierks in the southwestern part of the state about 2:40. Near the Rock Creek Bridge on Highway 70 the twister demolished three homes belonging to the Allen family. Six members of the family, representing four generations, perished. A seventh member of the community died nearby. From downtown Dierks school superintendent Leroy Gattis heard a terrific roar and saw a black funnel with the inside "like it was on fire." His first thought was of the consolidated school with almost 600 students. Fortunately, the storm turned northwest (the majority travel northeast or east), missing the school by only a few hundred yards. Mercifully, the time of day, when children were in school and many of the men were working at the Dierks Lumber and Coal Company, and the fact that many heard or saw the twister and headed for storm cellars kept the death toll from the F4 tornado low. When the winds subsided, stunned residents wandered through the uprooted trees and downed utility poles exchanging tales of narrow escapes and amusing anecdotes. Warned by the roar, Carl Young and his family, neighbors of the Allens, escaped injury by riding out the storm in their automobile parked in front of their house; the house was demolished. One man who had $100 tucked in his mattress rushed out of the storm cellar to find his home gone but the money still safely hidden.

The next community to feel the power of this tornado-producing thunderstorm was Paron in Saline County, thirty miles west of Little Rock. Many residents heard the tornado approaching and took shelter in storm cellars. Although a church, one home, and barns were destroyed and several homes were unroofed, Paron was lucky—there were no deaths or injuries. The storm churned northeastward through Faulkner County, producing an F2 tornado that destroyed small homes west of Mayflower and injured two people south of Saltillo.

The parent supercell that had produced the Dierks and Paron tornadoes gathered all its strength for its next victim, White County. Touching down about two miles southwest of Searcy, the monster tornado passed east of the county seat, home of Harding University. Following Highway 67 and the Missouri-Pacific Railroad tracks, the twister brushed the northwest edge of Kensett before plowing head-on into Judsonia at 5:34. The community of 1100 in the heart of Arkansas's strawberry country had no warning. Those who saw the storm said it was not a typical twisting, funnel-shaped tornado but a "huge green and black cloud moving across a wide front." When the roar subsided three minutes later, thirty citizens were dead and 95 percent of the town's buildings lay in various stages of ruin. A six-block area through the heart of town was completely obliterated.

Deadliest Day

The devastation was indescribable. *Commercial Appeal* photographer Rudolph Vetter who flew over the area the following day described the awful scene. "It looked like thousands of splinters had been spilled over the ground, but actually they were demolished houses and buildings." Pieces of clothing and sections of tin roofs hung from branches of the few trees left standing. Automobiles were buried under piles of rubble. Along the nine-block length of Judsonia's main street the wind had "pulverized sturdy brick business buildings and spewed out the rubble four or five feet deep." The city's water tank "was cracked open like an eggshell." Only the Methodist Church building remained relatively unscathed.

But the storm was not finished with White County. The next victim in the tornado's path was Bald Knob, a town of 2300 just seven miles northeast of Judsonia on U. S. Highway 67. When his television antenna toppled and a plank flew through a window, Mayor Jim Fletcher realized the storm was upon his community. In minutes the tornado killed ten and destroyed one-third of the residences and several businesses including two processing plants. One wall of the new school building was missing. The tornado moved northeastward from Bald Knob and claimed an additional life at Russell before it lifted into the clouds.

The tornado touched nearly every White County citizen. Fifty had died, including nine in rural areas of the county. Over 300 sustained injuries, and damage estimates approached $3.5 million. Those who personally had escaped the storm's destruction had a family member or friend who was not so fortunate. Along with the tallies of deaths and injuries came the personal tales of tragedy. Mrs. Vivian Spitzmesser of Copperas Springs, an employee of Robbins-Sanford Mercantile Company in Searcy, left work early to get home before the storm struck, but the tornado ended her life before she reached her destination. Ironically, she would have survived had she remained in Searcy. Only a few hours before the storm, twelve-year-old Edward Chapman had pitched Judsonia's sixth grade softball team to victory over the Morris School for Boys. He was one of the tornado victims. The W. E. Eadie family of Providence had come to Judsonia to sell strawberry plants, and seeing the approaching storm, they sought shelter in the Holmes Café. Taking a direct hit from the

Car buried under rubble in Judsonia. W. Irving Skipper.

Downtown Judsonia. W. Irving Skipper.

storm, the building crumbled killing Mrs. Eadie and her son Eddie. Mr. Eadie and another son Bobbie sustained serious injuries.

Searchers dug through the rubble for five hours hoping to find fifteen-year-old Glenda Fern alive, but their efforts were in vain.

For every sad account of loss of life there was a happy tale of escape from death or serious injury. Pool players in downtown Judsonia escaped injury by diving under the heavy tables. A brick and concrete counter at the Bus Station Café saved those who crouched under it. Twenty-two residents of Midway between Bald Knob and Judsonia crowded into Bratt Faulks's storm cellar. Mrs. Faulks had insisted that her husband build the shelter at their new home. The neighbors who had periodically kidded her about her "useless storm cellar" were not laughing when they escaped injury as the tornado demolished their homes.

The loss of life and destruction in White County was horrific, but Arkansas would suffer more before the day was over. At 5:26 a dark funnel cloud swooped to the ground in England, a town of 2500 in Lonoke County, twenty-two miles southeast of Little Rock. The tornado destroyed seven buildings in the west end of the business district before moving into the black residential section in the northwest part of town. Two blocks of frail residences disintegrated in the wind, leaving nine dead, 27 injured, and more than 200 homeless. As in the other tornadoes, everyone who survived had a story. Nathan Davis ran outside and lay down beside his car. The wind rolled him over and over, but he told reporters "the storm went over the car like the Lord was holding it back." Seventy-eight-year-old W. M. Eads, a veteran of five tornadoes, predicted Friday's twister and urged the Morrows, his daughter's family, to finish a storm cellar they had been building for weeks. They completed the work at 5 PM just in time for the family to escape the storm's fury. Fortunately, many people were not at home when the storm struck, and others knew of the approaching danger. Mayor Pat Henderson had received a warning of tornadic winds, and he and others passed the news along to those residents who had telephones. Mrs. Joe Foster, the wife of England's police chief, knew about the coming storm, but when it hit, she was "too stunned to think."

The England tornado, which some eyewitnesses described as "a perfect funnel," moved northeastward into Prairie County where it claimed two more victims. Still the tornado was not ready to lift back into the clouds. Passing just south of Hazen, it plowed across fields as it headed toward Cotton Plant, a town of 1800 on the southern edge of Woodward County. About 6 PM the twister roared through a relatively small area west and northwest of town, demolishing houses, strewing personal belongings across barren fields, wrapping cars around trees, overturning school buses, killing livestock, and even rolling wire fence into small balls like twine. Worst of all was the storm's impact on humans. Twenty-nine died, often several within the same family. All six members of the Albert Ingle family died when the tornado shattered their home about four miles southwest of Cotton Plant. The Antonio Galan family's six children also perished in the storm. More than 100 people suffered injuries serious enough to require hospitalization.

While the England-Cotton Plant tornado was destroying lives and property in southern sections of Lonoke, Prairie, and Woodruff counties, a parallel tornado was carving a path through the northern part of the same counties. Dipping to earth just southwest of Wattensaw, this tornado passed along the edge of that town before damaging parts of Hickory Plains, Georgetown, Patterson, and McCrory. Two died at Wattensaw, and two fatalities occurred at Hickory Plains. Continuing into Cross County, the twister killed four and destroyed thirty homes in Hickory Ridge then continued to Vanndale where it left behind substantial damage. After crossing Crowley's Ridge, the twister dissipated.

As the cold front inched eastward, additional tornadoes formed. One did minor damage when it skipped across Jackson, Poinsett, and Craighead Counties. A larger tornado that formed over Poinsett County about 6:45 damaged or destroyed twenty-one buildings in Fisher, killed two just north of Harrisburg, took an additional life at Trumann, and lifted near Blytheville after killing one in rural Mississippi County. The last Arkansas tornado fatality of that incredible day occurred when a short-lived twister etched a ten-mile-long path through Poinsett County from near Marked Tree to Lepanto. The storm system which spawned the deadly Arkansas outbreak finally moved eastward into the Missouri

Bootheel, Tennessee, and Mississippi where it produced eight tornadoes that killed ninety-two people.

Everywhere the tornadoes struck the story was the same. Law enforcement officials, college students, residents of surrounding areas, and the uninjured from the devastated communities dug through rubble, hoping to find survivors. Those lucky enough to survive the wind's onslaught were rushed to hospitals and clinics. At Dierks three Nashville physicians came to aid the town's lone doctor, Vale Harrison. The four treated the injured in Dr. Harrison's tiny office, but so many began to arrive in pickups, the doctors began treating them in the trucks' beds. One of England's first victims to arrive at Little Rock's Baptist Hospital, five-year-old Mose Tillman, Jr., was very fortunate there was one empty bed in the hospital's separate 41-bed black ward. Other black victims received treatment in the halls. The number of injured in White County was so great, workers set up additional medical facilities at Harding College, the National Guard Armory, and the Baptist Church when victims overwhelmed Searcy's two hospitals. Medical students from the University of Arkansas Medical School in Little Rock, interns from several hospitals, and even ordinary citizens cared for the injured.

During the next few days survivors struggled to overcome the shock of loss of family, friends, homes, and businesses, but they were not alone. The Arkansas National Guard aided in rescue work, traffic control, and cleanup and provided a necessary presence to discourage looting. Governor Sid McMath ordered the State Highway Department to send heavy equipment and dispatched convicts from the state penitentiaries to aid in debris removal. The Salvation Army and the American Red Cross rushed to the devastated areas immediately after the storms to aid volunteers in tending to the immediate needs of medical care, food, clothing, and shelter. The Red Cross allocated $1 million to Arkansas disaster relief and provided case workers to help the victims put their lives back together. No one could document the substantial amount of aid volunteers from various churches, civic organizations, and businesses from throughout the country provided those in need. On March 25 President Truman declared the storm-ravaged communities emergency disaster areas and allocated $700,000 for rebuilding schools, municipal buildings, and utilities.

The most heart-breaking task the survivors faced was burying the dead. At Judsonia three ministers conducted a joint funeral for eleven victims on the Monday morning following the tornado. Scores of volunteers had worked feverishly to remove limbs, branches, and downed trees from the Evergreen Cemetery in preparation for the mass burial. Throughout the storm-ravaged areas of the state the scene was repeated all too frequently. In Cotton Plant funerals were especially heart-wrenching. The town buried all six members of the Albert Ingle family on Saturday and the six Antonio Galan children on Sunday. With each funeral came a call for community members to renew their faith in God and start rebuilding their lives and towns.

Mennonite Disaster Relief Workers Helped to Rebuild Homes in Judsonia.

Chapter 3

Sharing the Deadliest Tornado Crown

Fort Smith (January 11, 1898) and Warren (January 3, 1949)

A comparison of Fort Smith in 1898 and Warren in 1949 would show glaring differences. Fort Smith, located on the Oklahoma border, was (and still is) the second largest city in Arkansas with an economy dependent upon transportation and trade. Warren in the southern Arkansas forests was an average-size town with an economy fueled by the lumber industry. Although the locations were vastly different, the tornadoes that struck were uncannily similar. Both (1) occurred in January, not the usual month for tornadoes in Arkansas, (2) received an F4 rating, (3) and were not the only tornado of the day in the state. The death toll from each tornado was identical, 55, but three of the fatalities from the storm that struck Fort Smith occurred across the Arkansas River in Crawford County; however, it was one continuous tornado, so the tornado has the distinction of being the single deadliest. Finally, both towns experienced another deadly tornado within a few years (Fort Smith in 1927 and Warren in 1975).

Fort Smith: January 11, 1898

It was hot, too hot for January. The temperature had soared to 78 degrees, well above the normal winter-time high, and the thermometer still registered 73 at 11 PM. The city was more crowded than usual that night. Federal court was in session, and farmers who had an interest in the proceedings filled the boarding houses or slept in their wagons in the wagon yards. The first indicators of an approaching storm that might bring some cooling rains were fast-moving bluish-green clouds and a light breeze that arose about 8 that evening. Seventy miles to the west a funnel cloud appeared between Hartshorne and Alderson in the Indian Territory, but lack of communications prevented the sleeping Arkansas town from receiving the news.

J. J. O'Donnell, the weather observer at Fort Smith, watched the approaching storm from his office at 608 Garrison Avenue and took extensive notes of the occurrence. He recorded frequent sheet lightning in the southern and western sky. Just after 11 PM while closing his office for the night, he heard a gurgling noise "like water rushing out of a bottle followed immediately by a rumbling, such as that made by a number of heavy carriages rolling rapidly over a cobblestone pavement, and finally like a railroad train." He rushed to the landing beneath the observatory's large skylight and saw a tornado 450 feet south of his position. O'Donnell described two "inverted siphons" that "came in contact with each other and twisted about one another downward to the ground." The highest wind speed the anemometer at his office recorded was sixty miles per hour.

The tornado first struck the city near the juncture of the Poteau and Arkansas Rivers before plowing into the national cemetery where the fierce winds collapsed the five-foot-high brick wall that surrounded the grounds, uprooted forty large oak trees, destroyed the keeper's residence, and lifted the concrete-embedded flag pole from the ground. After leaving the cemetery in utter ruins, the twister traveled eastward toward the heart of the city's business district. On the way, the storm blew through the cotton yards and displayed its capricious nature--it sucked the cotton from some of the bales but left the empty shells of burlap and metal loops intact. The storm reserved its greatest fury for the area along Garrison Avenue between Eighth and Twelfth Streets and a small area on Towson Avenue. Because it was night and the businesses were closed, the loss of life in this section of town should have been small, but several of the stores had living quarters above them. In addition, these blocks were home to hotels and boarding houses, many filled with visitors as well as permanent residents. The tornado continued eastward destroying family homes, church buildings, and small businesses. Near the end of its path, it seriously damaged the newly-built high school. After leaving a ten-mile long path of death and ruin, the funnel cloud crossed the Arkansas River and dissipated four miles east of Van Buren.

Two unwelcome companions to the tornado were fire and rain. After the winds passed, heavy rain fell upon the victims, adding to their misery and destroying their belongings that had survived the tornado's onslaught. In some cases this was a blessing because fires caused by overturned oil lamps compounded the tornado's destruction. A few who had escaped death from the tornado perished in fires. Men, women, and children, most in their night clothes, wandered the streets looking for relatives or seeking shelter from the elements. Within minutes those who had escaped the storm crowded into the stricken area to help rescue those buried under the rubble and provide aid to the displaced residents. The men in charge of the dead and wounded, led by Ernest M. Warren, faced a heart-breaking task as they encountered bodies clutching each other in death. Especially wrenching was their discovery of the bodies of Mr. and Mrs. Grayson, an aged couple well-known to the town's people, who faced death locked in each other's arms. Tears filled the eyes of the rescuers when they found children who looked like they were asleep but were dead. Thirty-three died immediately, and nineteen more would succumb to their injuries later. The official death toll in Fort Smith was 52, and the number of injured exceeded 100.

Firemen and medical personnel struggled to keep up with the demand for help. One of the nurses from St. John's Hospital, Miss Wood, tended to the injured who took refuge in the back of O'Keefe's saloon. Debris-clogged streets slowed the response of doctors and nurses, and downed telephone wires kept those in outlying areas from knowing the seriousness of the situation. To fill the void W. F. Germann opened his drug store on Garrison Avenue as an emergency hospital, and Ben Schaap dispensed free supplies from his drug store by candle light. The storm had toppled light poles, leaving the area in darkness. Once the city's doctors learned of the situation, they spread across the area and worked tirelessly without pay throughout the night and the days to follow.

Ruins of the new high school at Fort Smith. NOAA Photo Library.

Looking North on Reserve Addition showing the ruins in the cotton warehouse district in Fort Smith. NOAA Photo Library

Hundreds of buildings suffered destruction or heavy damage. Many students, unaware of the damage, reported for class at the city's new high school on the day following the tornado only to find their brand new school had a missing roof and caved in upper walls. The First Baptist Church and the Central Methodist Church were piles of rubble, and the Church of the Immaculate Conception had lost its spire. The home of the famous "Hanging Judge," Isaac Parker, was damaged beyond repair, and many of the judge's records were lost to history. Property damage exceeded $500,000 ($14 million in 2014 dollars). The next morning the mayor called a mass meeting of the citizens to provide relief for those who had suffered loss. Before they left the building, thousands of dollars had been donated, including substantial amounts from the Frisco and the Missouri Pacific Railroads. For days afterward items from Fort Smith were found throughout western Arkansas. A large photo of a young boy floated to earth near Clarksville, sixty miles to the east. A street sign from the corner of 13th and Garrison was found twenty-two miles away.

Much of the debris reached Ozark, thirty-five miles northeast of Fort Smith.

Many residents who survived the 1898 tornado were reminded of the horror of that storm when an F-3 rated tornado struck northeastern Fort Smith on April 12, 1927. The damage path, nearly four miles long and 150 yards wide, was about one-half mile east of the 1898 one. Two women perished and thirteen others required medical attention. The damage was relatively light; houses were unroofed, awnings and fences were blown down, and light buildings were knocked off foundations. This time two factors mitigated the losses: the storm struck in the daylight hours, and communications were better between Fort Smith and Oklahoma which suffered the brunt of the storms.

Warren: January 3, 1949

Record high temperatures blanketed heavily-forested southern Arkansas just three days into the new year of 1949. Workers returned to jobs after the New Year's holiday weekend. In Warren, a town of 2500 in Bradley County, that meant the Bradley Lumber Company which employed over 1000 men. In late afternoon an approaching cold front produced small tornadoes across northwestern Louisiana and counties to the north and southwest of Warren. After 5:30 continuous lightning and deafening thunder heralded the approach of a severe thunderstorm, and incessant rain and heavy hail obscured visibility. Few saw the "menacing black cloud centered by a reddish glow" sweep toward Warren, but most heard the roar described as "a dozen freight trains screaming over steel rails in the sky." The clock on the Bradley County Courthouse stopped at 5:43.

The tornado first touched down in far southwestern Warren and hopscotched its way across town, dipping to earth three more times to destroy homes and lives. The zigzag path, up to three-fourths-mile wide in sections, cut through predominantly residential areas. The major exception was the Bradley Lumber Company plant where winds crumpled the giant metal smokestack, demolished the power plant, and tossed heavy equipment about like children scatter toys on a Christmas morning. Left untouched were the stacks of lumber that covered several city blocks. People in many parts of town were unaware of the havoc that the storm was inflicting upon their neighbors until a power failure left the entire town in darkness. Immediately after the storm's cessation, residents of Warren grabbed flashlights and torches and began the arduous search through piles of rubble that had once been homes.

Warren did not have to face the disaster alone. Throughout the night ambulances from as far away as Memphis and Little Rock joined those from neighboring towns to transport the injured to hospitals in Monticello, El Dorado, and Little Rock. Doctors and nurses from towns throughout southeastern Arkansas aided their fellow medical workers from Warren in treating those with superficial injuries at the two Warren hospitals and emergency relief stations established at the YMCA building and the American Legion Hut. Arkansas Power and Light and the Army Corps of Engineers from Pine Bluff worked to restore power to essential facilities, and the Navy, McGorge Construction Company, and utility workers from throughout the state aided them in restringing the miles of electric and telephone wires the storm had left entangled in the piles of debris. The National Guard and State Police patrolled the stricken areas. The Little Rock Fire Department sent a truck and fifteen men to aid in extinguishing the fire at the Bradley Lumber Company. Licensed embalmers from southern Arkansas joined their counterparts at Frazer's Funeral Home to prepare the bodies of those who had succumbed to the tornado's fury. The day after the storm the governor sent prisoners from the Tucker Prison Farm to begin the clean-up process.

The next day survivors patiently stood in line to make long distance telephone calls to the outside world. One woman who had been waiting for hours told the person on the other end of the line to "tell mother we are all right and for her not to worry. We haven't got much of a house left, but we are okay." As news of the disaster spread around the country and overseas, relatives of residents of Warren tried frantically to reach them. When a young soldier stationed in Germany heard the news of the tornado, he called his in-laws to check on his wife; they didn't even know there had been a tornado. From Paris, France, a family member of

Mrs. Ernest Sangster inquired about her well-being. A daily newspaper in upstate New York used its resources to check on the welfare of their former employee who was the editor of the Warren *Eagle Democrat*. Too often though families who could not reach anyone to check on their relatives were forced to resort to long automobile trips; for some the information was heart-breaking, but for others the relief that their loved-one had survived was almost palpable.

As is true with every deadly tornado, the storm's treatment of the victims defied description. The F4 tornado with wind speeds estimated to exceed 200 miles per hour hurled people through the air, sometimes leaving them unrecognizable. Others were crushed beneath the roofs and walls of their homes. Warren school superintendent Perry Herring told the *Eagle Democrat* that "the destruction and the bodies piled in the Frazer garage is as bad as anything I saw at Chateau Thierry in World War I." Sadly, the Warren tornado claimed 55 lives, including entire families, and injured 400. As it wandered through neighborhoods where 1500 people lived, the twister destroyed 120 homes, severely damaged another 92, and left 500 houses in need of minor repairs. Two hundred families were left homeless. The monetary loss exceeded $1.35 million which included an estimated $85,000 loss to forests in the area.

Descriptions of the physical damage the tornado inflicted on the town filled every story of the tornado the *Eagle Democrat* published for more than a week. One described the devastation in the area around the Bradley lumber mill: "A bale of cotton, blown in from somewhere to the southwest, had caught in some broken timbers back of the sawmill and the flying cotton stuck to the fine wire fence surrounding the yard, giving the appearance of a million down feathers woven into a drapery on the fence." Some descriptions reinforced the intensity of the tornado. I-beams from the Bradley Lumber Mill that weighed tons appeared in yards several blocks away, and lumber from destroyed homes stood like picket fences in back yards untouched by the storm's fury. Heavy appliances like refrigerators were found several feet from any building site. Busses and cars were wrapped around trees like tinsel had wrapped around Christmas trees only a week earlier.

As usual, stories of odd occurrences surfaced. At the Pirtle home only the headboard complete with the locks for the side rails remained; the mattress, box springs, and side rails were gone. The capricious winds carried away Skeeter Hughes' garage but left his car and a child's toy that had been dropped on the floor next to it unscathed. Winds lifted one house from its blocks and set it down gently while others around it were unharmed. Near the beginning of its wanderings through the town, the twister blew the roof off a barn but left the lightweight hay untouched.

Every family in the stricken area had a heart-wrenching story to tell. Sometimes it was a description of their lost home and belongings, while others described their injuries or the frantic search for loved ones. The *Arkansas Gazette* related the story of one "doleful, sad-faced woman" who asked two state police patrolmen guarding the piles of rubble that had once been homes if she could search for some of her things. She told the officers that she had spotted her sewing machine and a quilt, but her house was several blocks away. The guards agreed that she could retrieve her belongings, and she thanked them with a forced smile. In the same article Kenneth Kelly, sitting in the debris of his destroyed home, told the reporter that the six people who had been in the house when the storm struck had been "scattered in all directions" but had survived with cuts and bruises, or as he phrased it were "all stove up." One of the sadder stories that appeared in the *Eagle Democrat* represented the despair of those who were searching for lost family members. Mrs. James McKinney, lying on a stretcher in the Hunt Hospital with serious injuries, pleaded to anyone who would listen to give her information on her children. She had found her oldest daughter in the wreckage of their home but could not locate her two younger children. Their bodies were later found at the morgue.

Funerals for the victims overwhelmed the local churches. Ministers from the Warren Ministerial Alliance lowered the barriers between denominations and shared the officiating role, sometimes in their own church building and sometimes in others or at graveside ceremonies. At the First Baptist Church the choir director led the choir in shifts throughout the day. Often funerals were for several members of one family. Seven children under the age of twelve were laid to rest; the Richard Dewberry family and James McKinney family lost two children each.

Help from various sources aided those who had lost property and jobs. Mayor Jim Hurley designated the American Red Cross as the official disaster relief agency and asked those citizens whom the tornado had not harmed to donate to the organization to help their fellow townspeople. Individuals and organizations throughout the state sent financial aid. The Arkansas Employment Security Division set up a special office in Warren to provide unemployment benefits to the many who had lost their jobs at the Bradley Lumber Company. Senators Fulbright and McClellan were instrumental in getting the Federal Works Administration to send temporary housing known as hutments. The Red Cross furnished these temporary shelters which were set up in the City Park.

A tornado can carry debris many miles. In the days and weeks following the storm articles were found as far away as Stuttgart, seventy-five miles northeast of Warren. A letter addressed to H.E. Green, a fatality of the tornado, and a history test paper belonging to eleven-year-old Patsy Curry were among those fragments of everyday life that residents near Stuttgart found and returned. A friend of the Ray Chathams, storm survivors, recognized the couple in a picture he found in his yard in Rock Springs, twenty miles from Warren. A coat belonging to Leonard Henderson, another storm fatality, fell to earth in a churchyard near Newton Chapel, thirty miles northeast of the stricken town.

The 1949 tornado was not the only deadly one to hit Warren. On March 28, 1975, another F4 twister followed much of its predecessor's path. Fortunately, this one took many fewer lives (seven) and injured sixty; unfortunately, the price tag was higher approaching $6 million. The lower fatality rate may be due to increased warnings and better built homes.

Chapter 4

The Deadliest Decade

Four Major Outbreaks in the 1920s

"The Roaring Twenties" was a decade when the winds of change blew through American culture and economics. In Arkansas the term had an additional meaning: literal winds roared through the state disrupting lives and changing forever the landscape of many small towns. More than 100 significant tornadoes (those that retroactively received a rating of F2 or higher or recorded at least one fatality) killed 383 during the 1920s, making this the deadliest decade in the state's history (see Appendix C for deaths by decade). Although the brunt of these storms focused on the central, north central, and eastern sections, no part of the state escaped, even the northwestern counties which rarely see tornado deaths.

April 15, 1921

The day had been warm and humid. The southern half of the state experienced temperatures between 70 and 80 and on-and-off-again thunderstorms. In mid-afternoon multiple tornadoes struck neighboring Texas where they killed eight before they roared across the state line. The deadliest twister of the day, at times up to a mile wide and packing F4 winds (over 200 miles per hour), carved a 70-mile long path through Miller, Hempstead, and Pike counties. The death toll from this one storm was 51 (16 in

Miller, 34 in Hempstead, and 1 in Pike), and property damage exceeded $2 million. Many of the dead were black tenant farmers who lived and worked on "plantations" in those southwestern counties. Especially hard-hit were the Trigenta and Shiloh communities and the Boyce, Sims, and Potter plantations in Miller County. In Hempstead County Sheppard, Dolph, Jackajones, Marlbrook, Wallaceburg, and Blevins received the storm's wrath.

As is true with every tornado, description of destruction defies words, survivor stories abound, and tales of oddities surface. At Shiloh home demonstration agent Lena Owens was conducting a meeting in the school building when the tornado destroyed the building around the attendees; none were seriously injured. W. S. Sims who lived 10 miles east of Texarkana gave a vivid account of the tornado. He said he saw a "great mass of leaves, timbers, and debris flying high in the air and in the distance a terrifying funnel." He rushed to his house and shouted for his wife and children to follow him to a nearby creek. The entire family escaped unharmed by crawling under a heavy concrete bridge; their home did not escape when the twister obliterated everything above ground. At the A.J. Brooks residence south of Blevins, the parents and their 11 children were buried under the rubble of their home, but no one was seriously hurt. They had huddled between 2 beds which had held the roof off them.

Not all stories had such a happy ending. At Wallaceburg searchers found 4 members of the Thebe Shackelford family and a visitor 100 yards from where their house had stood. The house had been lifted over the yard fence and scattered around the fifteen-acre homestead. Bodies of dead chickens and furniture lay tossed around like matchsticks; their car was found 200 yards from the home partially buried in the earth. Near Blevins Mrs. J.A. Duke and her children were in their small house when the tornado approached. She hurried her family to a neighbor's larger house that sat on a hill, thinking it would be safer. Mrs. Duke took her baby into a closet and held it in her lap to protect it from the storm. The twister blew a plank through the closet door and beheaded the poor woman; the baby was fine. While the twister had demolished the large house, the Duke house remained standing, virtually untouched.

Stories of unusual happenings, some which may be true and others which may be questionable, are abundant after tornadoes. Also near Blevins the twister demolished a church building but left the organ and the Bible. One family was sitting on their front porch when the storm struck. According to them, the tornado lifted their house from its foundation and blew it apart, but the porch on which they were sitting remained intact. None of them was injured. Money, some rolled neatly and held with a rubber band and some in small jars or banks, was found great distances from demolished homes.

Railroads cars are especially vulnerable to tornadic winds. Hempstead County Sheriff J.M. Dodson was on the Nashville-Hope train on the way to Little Rock with ten prisoners. While they were waiting at the station in Washington, a severe thunderstorm with constant lightning and hail struck. Suddenly green leaves and small twigs began falling from the sky. When the group boarded the train, they saw a red glow in the west which indicated the storm would soon be over. However, as the train moved eastward, the clouds became so dark the sheriff could see barely half-way down the passenger car. As the train pulled slowly out of Dolph, a huge piece of tin hit the side of the car, hail beat against the windows, and the wind howled fiercely. Within minutes the train stopped and passengers jumped out. Two cars loaded with cotton had blown off the track. The wind blew the engineer and fireman from the cab; the engineer believed that the engine had been lifted off the track and set back down without damage. A few houses and a barn along the track were piles of rubble, but no one had sustained an injury. After a short delay, the track was cleared and the shaken passengers resumed their journey.

Governor McRae's response to the devastation was similar to other disasters of this time. No federal relief programs existed. No state relief went to the hard-hit areas; the state coffers had exhausted all of their funds that had to cover floods, droughts, and tornadoes. The governor, however, did orderer the National Guard to send tents and cots to Blevins, but individual citizens and local charities such as churches would have to provide for those in need. Many relief workers from Hope brought clothes and food paid for by the citizens of the town and aided in the search for victims.

Smaller less destructive tornadoes struck Yell, Pope, and Pulaski Counties. One fatality occurred in Gravelly (Yell County) when the home in which he was a visitor disintegrated in the violent winds. Four people died in one home in Pope County when an F3 tornado destroyed several homes near Appleton. Two tornadoes in Pulaski County left behind considerable damage but no fatalities and few injuries.

November 25, 1926

Many Americans had celebrated this Thanksgiving Day with a family feast and a remembrance of what God had provided for our country and for them. Arkansans were no different, but before the day ended many would be thanking God as well for sparing their lives. Fourteen significant tornadoes killed fifty-nine of the state's residents and left hundreds homeless as they hopscotched across the central part of the state from north to south.

At 5:00 PM the first deadly tornado claimed two lives in Pope County. Fifteen minutes later an F3 twister plowed its way from northeastern Pope County into Conway County where it killed three near Old Hickory and Macedonia, then moved into Van Buren County where it claimed three more lives near Choctaw. At virtually the same time another tornado, this one a powerful F4, moved from Faulkner County (one died at Enders) into neighboring Cleburne County, devastating a town that a deadly twister had struck only ten years before—Heber Springs.

After the 1916 tornado many citizens of the Heber Springs area built storm cellars. When threatening weather rolled into their town at the dinner hour, those who had prepared to escape a future tornado ran to their shelters. This kept the death toll down when the monster tornado first struck the Edmonson addition in the southwestern part of town then continued northeastward, devastating a fifteen-block area. In its wake the twister left uprooted trees, smashed cars, crushed homes, and twenty-two fatalities.

Some residents reported seeing a funnel cloud pass overhead twenty minutes before the main storm struck although an *Arkansas Gazette* account said that the storm struck "with a suddenness that dazed the population." An overcast sky, heavy drops of rain, and hail preceded the "low hum in the distance" which heralded the arrival of the tornado. Those who recognized the sound as an approaching tornado hurried to storm cellars. Some such as the Price Riddle family were not able to reach shelter in time. The family rented a house from Ben Treas. When they realized that a tornado was approaching, they ran for the Treas' cellar but decided to stop at the Treas' house to see if it was alright to do so. As the family of six was climbing the steps to the home (they did not know that the Treas family had already gone to the shelter), the storm struck and obliterated the house. One-year-old C.C. died instantly; the remainder of the family sustained serious injuries, and the father (Price) later died in a Little Rock hospital. Price's wife Almeda became a well-known folk song writer and singer. Price's brother and his family escaped injury when their house was destroyed; little Seattle Elizabeth was so terrified of storms she insisted the family go to the storm cellar before the tornado hit. The winds picked up the Richardson Building and hurled it into the street where it caught fire. Seven members of the Parker family who were inside perished.

After the twister left Heber Springs, the town faced numerous problems. Downed power lines left the entire area in darkness. Searchers used lanterns to hunt for victims. Fires broke out in some of the ruins, but torrential rains that followed the winds quenched many before they could spread. Sheriff Emmett Baldridge sustained a serious foot injury while searching for victims but remained in charge of caring for the injured, even when he had to prop his foot up on his desk. The number of injuries far exceeded the ability of the Heber Springs doctors to handle. The station agent for the Missouri and North Arkansas Railroad telegraphed neighboring towns for help, and nurses and doctors from Searcy began arriving within two hours. Railroad cars transported the most seriously injured to Little Rock. The Cleburne County Courthouse became a hospital where doctors performed surgery under the dim lights of lanterns as family members milled about hoping for a positive word. Rescuers dug through the rubble throughout the night in search of victims. When Olmstead Mortuary had no more room, the second floor of the courthouse served as an additional morgue. National Guard units cleared the streets and buried animal carcasses to prevent contamination of the city's wells.

Henry Dorris, a reporter for the *Arkansas Democrat*, flew into the town the next morning. Viewing the ruins from the air, he reported that it appeared as if a giant mowing machine had run across the town. From Spring Park to the center of town all that he saw was destruction; houses, churches, and business buildings no longer lined the streets. Only the Methodist Episcopal Church survived intact. The only business functioning the day after the tornado was the drug store, a necessity.

As they had done just ten years earlier, citizens of Heber Springs who escaped the storm's wrath aided those who were not as fortunate. Many opened their homes to those in need of shelter, and all of the local eating establishments stayed open around the clock to provide food and coffee for victims and relief workers alike. Neighboring communities provided aid of various kinds, and the town officials designated the Red Cross as the organization to provide long-term aid. The $500,000 damage estimate for this storm ($6.6 million in 2015) far exceeding that of the first one to hit Heber Springs. Fortunately, the death toll did not.

Less destructive storms pummeled areas near Belleville (Yell County), Mountain Home (Baxter County), Arkadelphia (Clark County), Jessieville (Garland County), and Portland (Ashley County); none claimed a life. The same cannot be said about a second tornado of the day to strike Conway County. Five died south of Opello. One child died south of Sheridan (Grant County), two died between Newport and Jacksonport (Jackson County), and three perished near Gould (Lincoln County).

Other than the tornado that struck Heber Springs, the deadliest storm of the day occurred in Jefferson County. Ten died and 40 sustained injuries when an F3 twister carved a six-mile-long path of destruction through the southeastern part of the county near the community of Moscow. Sadly, what should have been a happy day turned into a tragedy when the tornado touched down at the Good Hope Baptist Church on the Nickerson plantation. A large crowd had assembled at a wedding in the building. As they were leaving, the tornado demolished the building and scattered bodies about. Members of the wedding party as well guests were victims.

Near the end of its life, the thunderstorm complex that produced the death and destruction struck a final death blow. A twister that formed in Louisiana crossed the border into Arkansas where it killed one oil field worker and five people in one house in Columbia County. The final storm of the day left three dead near Gould in Ashley County. The six hours that the storms had ravaged the state left millions of dollars in damages in sections of 16 counties.

May 9, 1927

Seventy Arkansans died and more than 400 suffered injury when seven deadly tornadoes (four additional ones caused no deaths) swooped down on the state on this Monday in late spring. Arkansas did not suffer alone on this deadly day, however. Before dawn tornadoes killed 40 in the Dallas area, and Missouri endured one of that state's deadliest tornado strikes when ninety-three perished in Poplar Bluff. Illinois lost eight citizens, and Louisiana counted one death. By the day's end 28 significant tornadoes (those rated F2 or higher or caused a death) touched down in the country's midsection claimed 212 lives and left behind hundreds of injured and millions of dollars' worth of property damage.

The harbinger of the day's storms was a small, weak (F2) tornado that touched down briefly shortly after noon in northeast Faulkner County where it destroyed a house and a barn near Beckett Mountain but killed or injured no one. More than 1 ½ hours passed before the second tornado of the day dropped out of the sky near Scott in Pulaski County; no one was killed, but seven were injured. Mother Nature was just warming up, however. From 2:30 to 4:30 parent thunderstorms that exploded over the northeastern and southern parts of the state produced unwanted children that left death and destruction in their paths. A tornado or possibly up to three separate ones killed two near Carlisle (Lonoke County) and six at Center Point in Prairie County. About the same time a twister that tracked across parts of Lawrence and Randolph counties destroyed 15 homes and killed five near Maynard and Brockett before taking aim at Poplar Bluff.

Lawrence County was not finished with tornadoes for the day, however. As the hour for school dismissal approached (3 PM), a devastating twister struck the southwest side of Hoxie where the brand new high school stood. The storm smashed the third floor and the gym; two students were instantly killed and several injured by the falling debris. Roaring on, the tornado struck the elementary school, three blocks from the high school. There the story had a better ending. Although the school lost its second floor, no students were seriously injured. Following a path through town, the twister blew the Frisco train, waiting at the depot, on its side. James Bland of Walnut Ridge and his wife and children were waiting in their car at the depot when the storm struck. He saw the winds flip over three cars of the passenger train he had intended to board and blow a wagon and team of mules down the street. He grabbed his children and rushed into the depot; they escaped injury. In a whimsical manner the twister had demolished the depot and overturned the train sitting on the tracks but left untouched the four-story hotel that adjoined the depot. Destruction was everywhere. More than 100 buildings were heavily damaged or destroyed. In addition to the students, nine others died (five in one family and four in another), 200 received injuries, and property damage totaled $300,000.

Farther south, a weaker tornado (F2) leveled homes near Toledo and Randall in Cleveland County. The death toll (nine) might have been higher, but the area had a warning--a stiff wind preceded the twister, and the roar could be heard at a great distance. The northeast quadrant of the state was still in danger though. An F3 twister cut a 27-mile long path from near Egypt

(Craighead County) to Stanford (Greene County); part of the path went through Lawrence County, the third storm to hit them that day. John Rich was in Egypt when he saw the tornado approaching his home only a short distance outside the town. He ran to warn his wife and children, but before he could arrive the tornado demolished the house and killed his wife, his five children, and a visiting neighbor child. Searchers found the body of twelve-year-old Doyle Brown in a tree 100 yards from where he had been working in a field; he survived until morning. Of the ten deaths near Egypt, eight were children. At Pierce Hill a mother and child died, but a seven-month old baby survived as winds shattered their home. More tornadoes hopscotched around the state that afternoon. Brief touchdowns occurred near Kingston in Madison County and Bethesda in Independence County.

Although twisters visited sixteen counties on May 9, the county to suffer the most deaths was in an area of the state not known for tornadoes—Union County on the Louisiana border. At 3:30 a brief F2 tornado (the path was only two miles long) burst out of the clouds over the village of Norphlet. Fortunately, the winds struck just before school was to be dismissed; the children remained inside and all escaped injury. A menace not usually encountered in a tornado is collapsing oil derricks, but one crashed into a wing of the hospital, buried an ambulance, and injured two nurses while other derricks fell on houses. Most of the damage was in the residential area; one person died. The final tornado of the day was the deadliest and most destructive. All of the previous storms had alerted Superintendent W.M. Bingham to the potential of a tornado hitting Strong. As a precaution he ran from classroom to classroom telling students to "hurry home. A storm is coming." Most paid no attention though. Tommie Lee Gorman headed for his after-school job at the family grocery store, and others went about their usual business. Mary Burgess and Mary Spenser headed for the Spenser law office to get a ride home. Mr. Spenser and his friend Gill Johnson climbed the outside stairs of the building to get a better idea of why a strange darkness had fallen on the town. They saw the girls coming up the street and a black funnel cloud to the southwest. Spenser ran to catch the girls and get them to safety. He hurried them into the office and told them that a storm was coming and they had to stay together. As they glanced out the window, they saw the Barbee Motor Company explode and a thick oak tree fly past. Before they knew it, Spenser and the two girls were hurled through space along with all of the debris. They came to rest on a pile of bricks in the middle of the street. Hurrying to escape the torrential rain and hail, they found shelter in the partially destroyed hardware store. At the railroad station A. A. Eudy continued telegraphing for help until the telegraph line became a victim of the wind. Help arrived quickly from El Dorado. Searchers began the grim task of looking for survivors and recovering bodies of the dead. One who perished was Tommie Gorman. Long after the storm had gone, rescuers dug Helen Williams from under the pile of rubble that had once been the Williams Rexall Drug Store. She had suffered a broken arm and a skull fracture but had survived. Five others, including her mother and two-year-old sister, had not been as fortunate. Rube Duck and his father waited to be rescued from beneath the ruins of their family livery stable. The elder Duck cried out, "Rube, help me, I'm dying." Trying to console his father, Rube replied, "Don't worry Papa. Everyone else in Strong is dead too." He was obviously wrong, but 24 citizens of the town did die in the tornado; 72 others suffered injury. The entire business area as well as many large homes were gone. Damage estimates reached $500,000.

El Dorado, the county seat about twenty miles northwest of Strong, went into action immediately. A special train, ambulances, and even private cars rushed the injured to the El Dorado hospital. Seventy-five members of the local American Legion post went to Strong to search for survivors and help clear the streets, and the chamber of commerce joined with the Salvation Army to send stoves and provide hot meals and coffee for those the twister had driven from their homes. Half of El Dorado's police department and all of the sheriff's department aided in keeping order. The town's hotels gave relief workers a place to stay.

On Wednesday a mass funeral service was held on the town square; stricken families buried their loved ones in several different cemeteries. Many of the victims who were family members of prominent citizens of El Dorado were interred in that town. An especially touching event occurred a few weeks after the tragedy. The senior class of Strong High School joined the El Dorado High School graduates for a joint commencement ceremony at the latter's school. One chair, draped in black, stood empty in honor of Tommie Lee Gorman.

April 10, 1929

F5 (and the new designation EF5) tornadoes are rare. While the neighbors to the west (Texas and Oklahoma) can each claim several of the strongest tornadoes (Oklahoma leads the nation), Arkansas has had only one tornado reach the designation, the April 10, 1929, twister that leveled the community of Sneed in Jackson County. (NOTE: Tornadoes before 1950 were classified by reviewing photographs and newspaper accounts of the destruction.)

Eight tornadoes, four of them deadly, swarmed across the northeast quadrant of the state on the afternoon and evening of a day which had been warm and sultry. In their paths they left 55 dead, more than 200 people seriously injured, and approximately $1 million in damages. The first tornado that touched down near Calico Rock (Izard County) about 3 PM caused little destruction except to timber. A similar weak twister occurred about 4:30 at Mt. Pleasant; it, too, left behind little damage. But it seemed that the atmosphere was being primed for bigger and more destructive storms.

The first deadly tornado struck Harpel where two fatalities occurred before it roared into Guion (Izard County), a mining community of 400 people along the White River in the Ozark foothills. Many residents were employees of the Silica Products Company. As housewives were preparing dinner, a tornado carved a half-mile-wide path down a mountain, across the White River, through the town, and back up another mountain. All that remained when the storm moved on were three houses that served as shelter for the wounded. Even the concrete-block Izard County Bank was a pile of rubble, and the vault had been torn open. One resident remarked to the *Arkansas Democrat*, "It took 20 years to build and four minutes to tear down." Hershell Stephens, principal of the Guion School, related a typical survivor story. After letting out school at the usual time of 4:00, he ran some errands in town. When he saw the tornado approaching, he took his wife and baby to a storm cellar, but it was full. The couple returned home. While holding the baby, he felt the house fall around him. Twice the winds forced the baby from his arms, but he was able to recover the child. Stephens suffered a knee injury, but the child was unhurt. Similarly, Harry Teague held a baby as his house disintegrated around him. He was bruised but the baby was fine. Seven perished in Guion, and property damage exceeded $165,000.

Two tornadoes formed close to each other near Almond in Cleburne County and moved northeastward. Observers near Batesville who were watching the storm thought it was one tornado that split into two when it reached the White River, one moving eastward toward Moorefield (Independence County) and the other moving northeasterly toward Jackson County. The first twister injured ten and left behind $20,000 damage in Moorefield. The other one did little damage until it seemingly exploded over the community of Sneed, 3 miles north of Swifton (Jackson County). This tornado, the only one in Arkansas history to receive an F5 designation, killed 23, seriously injured 32, and destroyed $155,000 of property. How was the F5 designation determined? Tom Grazulis, a tornado researcher and statistician who rated tornadoes that occurred in the United States from 1880 to 1950, told the *Dallas Morning News* that "It was such complete obliteration, with so many deaths, it just seemed to warrant the absolute maximum ratings." He considered the Sneed tornado (sometimes called the Swifton tornado) to be the deadliest of the year. He continued by saying "Totally swept away is the criteria for F-5. Ordinarily you have a single house swept away and the tornado becomes F-5. Here you have an entire community." Some seventy years after the Sneed tornado, the Little Rock National Weather Service office officially confirmed the F-5 rating.

Several stories of the Sneed tornado confirm its power. Nona Campbell, who was ten years old at the time of the tornado, remembered her father's horses being thrown across their farm and hail as big as a hand. Lones Eldridge, eleven at the time of the storm, told the *Dallas Morning News*: "I know I'm going to heaven, because I've spent my hell." He also described the tornado's actions by saying "It took those houses up 500 feet. They'd shrink in and explode like they was a half-mile wide." Lucille Tucker Burkett related the tornado story about her family which had been told to her (she was three at the time of the storm) in the *Woodruff County Historical Society Journal*. Her father and Cleo Nicholson, a close neighbor, had gone to the White River to set out trout lines. Lessie Nicholson stayed at the Tucker home to visit with Pearl Tucker, her two daughters, and Pearl's mother. About 5:00 Cleo asked Reuben if that was smoke from a train on the horizon. When they looked closer, the men realized that it was a tornado coming toward them. As they ran to the house, they saw the women running outside. They yelled over the noise of the approaching tornado to run to the Nicholson's home which they thought was sturdier and could withstand the winds better. On the way they urged the John Loy family to join them. From a window the twelve watched the twister demolish the Tucker's house and barn. As the storm approached the Nicholson's house, the southwest corner blew away and the garage came flying into the house. Those inside the house ran to another room for refuge; some were crying and some were screaming. Witnesses who saw the storm hit the house reported that the last remaining room was carried ten or twenty feet into the air where it exploded, dumping its occupants into a muddy field. The Nicholsons, the Loys, and Mrs. Rowlett (Mrs. Tucker's mother) died. The rest were injured. Years later Mrs. Burkett remembered seeing the kitchen range "sail from the kitchen and out the back door." Not far away, five members of the Charles Defries family died; some of the bodies were recovered from a drainage ditch a distance from where their home had stood. A few in Sneed escaped death by taking refuge in unusual places. The Arthur Smiths huddled under a chicken coop; the storm destroyed their shelter but left them unharmed. Jim

Swink and seven members of his family hid under a bridge; the storm destroyed their home, but they were safe. Before ambulances could take the injured to Newport for treatment, roads had to be cleared of downed trees and debris that blocked all the roads. A temporary morgue was set up in a vacant building in Swifton.

This storm cellar in the Sneed Community saved lives during the F5 tornado. NWS

The third killer of the day left behind 8 fatalities, 30 injured persons, and $150,000 in property damage in the Lorado community (Greene County). Seven members of the Lowthorp family perished when the twister scattered their home over several acres; only one member of the family, eleven-year-old Lizzie, survived. The final tornado of the day formed southwest of Wynne in Cross County about 8 PM. At Smith's Chapel the storm claimed one life and injured 37 before moving into Princedale. Fifteen died in the area, including all eight members of the Perry Graham family who lived east of Wynne in the St. Francis bottom near Princedale. Four members of the J. L. Lucas family which included two small children were also victims of the storm. Following Highway 64, the twister killed one and injured four at Parkin before dissipating. Property damage from this tornado was $250,000. Residents of the counties that smaller tornadoes had visited (Cleburne, Independence, Craighead, and Lawrence) were thankful that they had been spared the unfortunate events that had struck so many of their Arkansas neighbors.

Chapter 5

The Deadliest Year in the Modern Era: 1968

Jonesboro, May 15 and Greenwood, April 19

The year had been quiet. Only one tornado, rated a weak F0, had struck anywhere in Arkansas during the first three months of the year, but April and May would change a quiet tornado year into the state's deadliest in modern times (since 1953). Sixty-five would perish, and 723 would be injured, most in two tornadoes that struck cities on opposite sides of the state: Greenwood on the western border and Jonesboro in the northeastern quadrant.

Greenwood: April 19

The severe weather system that produced two weak tornadoes in Oklahoma moved across the border in mid-afternoon on Friday. The 2,016 residents of Greenwood were unaware of the potential danger that loomed on their doorstep. School dismissed at its usual time of 3:00. Shoppers and those who had city or county business milled around the town square (Greenwood is one of the two county seats of Sebastian County). Those who were paying attention to the weather said that the sky turned "an eerie green-black color." Seemingly without warning the all-too-familiar roar of a tornado announced the monster's appearance at 3:15. In less than five minutes an F4 tornado killed 14, injured 270, and left the town square in shambles. Although it was on the ground for only two miles, the twister left behind unbelievable damage. An Arkansas state trooper said the devastation looked like "the aftermath of World War II bombing raids." The city's mayor, Ed Hall, estimated that two-thirds of the town was destroyed. The heaviest damage was around the square. The bell tower and third story of the court house had toppled into the street. Most of the deaths were in the residential area in the southwestern part of town. The cost of the tornado was $1.5 million.

The death toll might have been higher had the twister struck at a different time of day. Many students had already left the high school when the winds hit. Students in a study hall had taken shelter in a hallway only seconds before the walls fell in. Others lay on the floor when they saw the tornado approaching. None were injured. Fatalities were also reduced because many residents worked in Fort Smith, twelve miles to the north; they were not home at the time of the tornado.

Within minutes help came from surrounding communities in Oklahoma and Arkansas. Ambulances streamed in to take the dead and injured to hospitals in Fort Smith and Van Buren. The Red Cross brought in medical personnel to treat the less severely injured on site. Marine reservists who were training at nearby Fort Chaffee directed traffic and guarded against looting. Linemen from several towns worked on restoring electricity and telephone service. By Saturday morning they had six functioning telephones at the Greenwood telephone office that allowed residents to contact friends and relatives. Two Fort Smith dairies hauled water into town until the water system was up and running again. Truckloads of needed supplies flowed in from people in both states.

Wilma Cabe told reporters she had left her two young sons with her mother while she went to the beauty shop but she would not have left them if she thought that a tornado would hit. When the winds howled, she and the other women in the shop took shelter in a storage room. Her mother and sons along with Wilma's grandparents hid in a basement storage unit underneath her grandparent's home. Debris from the crumbling house badly injured them; her grandfather did not survive.

Sandra Traylor was in Fort Smith when the tornado struck. When she heard about the storm, she grabbed her husband and children and headed toward Greenwood. After several detours they got close enough to town to walk in through the destruction. She reported that it seemed to her that nobody knew what to do—they were lost and in shock. When she reached her parents' home, Sandra was surprised by the capricious nature of the twister. The winds had flattened one house and left the next intact, then repeated the pattern down the road.

Doug Kinslow was a fourth-grader walking home when the tornado struck. He grabbed a holly bush, and he recalled holding on to it when his feet left the ground as the winds blew him sideways. A neighbor saw him and put him into his car to wait out the storm. When the winds stopped, Doug walked on toward home, or at least where he thought it was. All that remained was a big pile of rubble and parts of a wall. His mother and father and one sister had survived uninjured. His mother had some poke sallet soaking in the sink; it was still there, but the kitchen that had been around it was gone. They had been in the house just nineteen days. His father's barber shop was destroyed, and the family car lay on top of Mayor Hall's truck.

In the days before Doppler radar, warnings relied upon spotters in the field notifying authorities of a tornado on the ground. Because this tornado developed right on top of Greenwood, there was little advanced warning; however, it had a unique spotter—a space satellite. NASA had developed Application Technology Satellites (ATS) to directly benefit mankind. The space agency partnered with the National Oceanic and Atmospheric Administration (NOAA, parent of the National Weather Service) in 1968 to use the satellites for hurricane tracking. In early 1968 one of the satellites was put in orbit over the central United States. It continually photographed the earth during daylight hours when a tornado watch was in effect. The goal was to provide a better understanding of tornado formation. The ATS 3 satellite captured the Greenwood tornado as it was destroying the town.

Jonesboro: May 15

Children are often afraid of the dark. They think they see monsters that will hurt them. Parents assure them that they have nothing to fear—the monsters are not real. But, the children were right on the night of May 15, 1968. A horrible monster lurked in the dark, ready to pounce on the unsuspecting people of northeastern Arkansas.

Conditions were ripe for a major outbreak on May 15. In mid-afternoon the first tornado touched down in Minnesota, and the storm system progressed southward. At 8:12 PM the U.S. Weather Bureau issued a tornado watch for an area from Harrison, Arkansas, to Belleville, Illinois, and at 9:20 they issued a second watch for an area from 45 miles south of Walnut Ridge, Arkansas, to Owensboro, Kentucky.

About 6:30 PM the first Arkansas tornado of the evening struck Mountain Home in Baxter County where it destroyed twenty homes, damaged fifty others, and claimed three lives. The short-lived twister, rated an F3 on the Fujita scale, damaged boats, boat docks, and resort homes on Lake Norfolk before dissipating near the community of Henderson.

Two hours later, an F-4 tornado roared through Oil Trough in Independence County, destroying two-thirds of the town of 235 residents. The post office and grocery store were demolished, and the high school, an implement business, and numerous cars suffered heavy damage. At the Church of Christ Wednesday evening services were in progress. The sixty people inside the building heard the approaching storm and took cover under pews. Although the structure, directly in the path of the tornado, exploded around them, only one suffered serious injuries; no one died at the church, but five in the community perished and fifty were injured. The total damages at Oil Trough were $750,000.

The third deadly tornado of the night came to life at Tuckerman (Jackson County) at 8:45 where it left behind one fatality, twenty damaged or destroyed homes, and a few damaged businesses on the south side of town. Under cover of darkness the monster twister barreled forward at 30 mph toward Jonesboro, the largest city in northeastern Arkansas and home to Arkansas State University (ASU) and its 6000 students. Darkness and rain obscured the tornado cloud, giving residents little warning as it approached. Residents who were awake about 9:45 might have heard its roar or seen the outline of the cloud when lightning flashes lit up the sky. The tornado followed a twelve-mile long path from Valley View, across the southern part of Jonesboro, and into Fairview and Nettleton. Everywhere it went, the narrow (at most points one-fourth to one-half mile wide) F4 twister left behind death and devastated lives. After leaving Jonesboro, the twister lifted for a short distance then touched down again in downtown Manila (Mississippi County), where it destroyed twelve buildings but no lives were lost.

As soon as the storm passed, rescue efforts began. Police estimated that 1000 college and high school students worked feverishly through the night as they sought survivors, often rescuing them from beneath piles of rubble. Fallen electrical wires, uprooted trees blocking streets, and a heavy rain that followed the storm hampered their efforts. ASU students frequently used their own blankets they had brought from their dorms to wrap up the injured and transported them to the hospital for treatment where they helped set up cots and ran errands. The mayor told the Jonesboro Sun "you can bet I was proud of them." Taxi driver Woody Hatton drove his nurse wife to the hospital then provided transportation for other nurses and victims to emergency treatment sites. Governor Winthrop Rockefeller order 400 National Guardsmen into the ravaged areas to provide whatever assistance was necessary. Unfortunately, not everyone who came to the tornado-damaged areas was there to help. Within an hour of the storm's passing, looters appeared to take advantage of the unfortunate citizens who had lost homes and businesses. Sheriff's deputies and guardsmen were taken away from rescue efforts to arrest looters. On Saturday local and state officials were forced to issue a warning that any unauthorized person found in the devastated area would be arrested on the spot and taken to jail.

Immediately after the storm, St. Bernard's Hospital was overwhelmed with the injured. Scores of volunteers worked throughout the night to set up a make-shift hospital at the Jonesboro National Guard Armory. Doctors came from throughout the state as well as from Tennessee and Missouri. Two doctors from Searcy, where Jonesboro doctors had helped with the injured after a devastating tornado in March 1952 struck the area, came to Jonesboro to return the favor. Veteran doctors called the scene at the local hospital the worst they had ever seen. Fifty of the injured, several of them critically wounded, were taken to Memphis. Sadly, the Craighead County Coroner had to establish a temporary morgue at the Community Center where volunteers aided the law-enforcement officials with forms and identification of the fatalities. One volunteer, Sargent Homer Talley, the Jonesboro Marine Recruiter and veteran of several military campaigns, told the *Jonesboro Sun*: "I have seen many people dead at one time on the battlefield. But that can't compare with the scene on the floor of this gym. This is the most I have ever see dead at one time." The final death toll at Jonesboro climbed to thirty-four. This in itself is a major tragedy, but even worse was the fact that a staggering number of the dead were children. Twelve were age twelve and under; sixteen were under age eighteen. In several families both a parent and at least one child died.

As is usual after a deadly storm, survivor's stories filled the newspapers and airwaves. Many came from the Nettleton community, one of the hardest hit areas. John Foltz told the *Arkansas Democrat*: "I just stood in the doorway of our bedroom until everything was gone." He explained that he and his wife were getting ready for bed when they heard the roar of the approaching tornado. She hid between the mattress and box springs. This saved her life when the room caved in on top of the bed. He had been standing on the only part of the floor still in the room after the tornado moved their house a foot or two. Foltz said he believed the tornado lasted about 30 seconds. Mrs. Foltz was shocked to see that the twister had moved the house only a few feet because it seemed to her that the storm was moving the house a great distance. Mrs. Dallas Scallions, jumped under the bed when she

65

heard the storm coming, but her husband was knocked unconscious before he could reach shelter. Although she lost her false teeth, neither was seriously injured. Marvin Higgins told the same reporter that he and thirteen others had escaped injury by squeezing into a storm cellar as outside the twister demolished their homes and tossed vehicles about like toys. The report of what he saw when he and the others emerged is a sample of the heart-breaking scene. "When I came out, people had been blown into their yards and were screaming for help. I found a man and his wife lying in my yard. He died during the night, and the hospital said this morning that she wasn't expected to live." He found two victims, a man and child, dead in a car behind his house. Joel and Phil Phillips survived when they dived under the snack bar as their house crashed around them. Phil described the sound as like a train coming through the house and a big explosion, and his brother said it sounded like someone threw a bomb at the house.

Johnny and Delena Brown, a young Fairfield couple with two children, gave a vividly detailed account of the tornado from two different perspectives. When the lights went out about 9:45, Johnny and his -year-old son went to the store to get some candles while Delena stayed home with their three-month-old daughter. When the wind picked up and objects began hitting the side of the house, Mrs. Brown began to worry and ran to look out the front door to see what was happening. At that moment, the brick wall to their carport collapsed against the side of the house. Delena ran to pick up her baby and crouched with her in a corner of the room while the winds roared and the house shook around them. She sneaked a peak out the window and saw the electric wires in the backyard sparking. Terrified, she prayed as the flashes from the power line illuminated the room. The prayers for her and her baby were answered—they escaped harm, but just a hundred yards from her back door lay eight bodies, fatalities of the horrific storm. While Delena and the baby were riding out the storm in their home, Johnny and their son were caught in their car. The winds blew out the automobile's right front window and the right front tire off its rim, but Mr. Brown was determined to get home to see if his wife and baby had survived. On his way he had to detour around a new home that was in the middle of the road. When he got home, relief flooded over him. Although the tornado had blown off the roof and heavily damaged the house, the room where Delena and his daughter had taken shelter was the only one in the structure that escaped untouched; the baby slept throughout the entire ordeal.

Aid seemed to come from everywhere. The Salvation Army, the Red Cross, and local churches and organizations hurriedly set up emergency relief stations throughout the devastated area. Many communities, including the city of Memphis (TN), and churches throughout Arkansas and Tennessee provided monetary aid as well as workers to help in the cleanup effort. The National Guard and state police patrolled the streets; city and county workers worked around the clock to clear streets; utility workers from surrounding areas aided their Jonesboro compatriots in returning electricity and gas to the hard-hit communities. Senator J. William Fulbright told reporters as he toured the area, "This makes your own problems seem small." He and federal officials got a first-hand view of the tornado-stricken sites to access damage and offer encouragement to the survivors. Fulbright and Arkansas Governor Winthrop Rockefeller urged the federal government to send financial aid. President Lyndon Johnson sent a telegram to the governor to express his distress at the loss of life and to ensure him that the federal government would do everything it could to assist in the emergency.

Estimated property losses were $8 million in 1968 dollars (over $53 million in 2014) which included 164 homes completely destroyed and hundreds of others damaged. The Nettleton schools were hit especially hard; the elementary school was destroyed and the high school received extensive damage. More than half the county's cotton crop was lost, but dry weather would enable replanting.

Jonesboro had never had a tornado death before May 1968. Ironically, the city suffered another devastating tornado on May 27, 1973, which left behind more significant damage than the earlier one, but fortunately claimed only three lives, two in the rural community of Otwell eight miles southwest of Jonesboro and one within Jonesboro city limits. Like its predecessor, this twister struck in the dark. The 1973 tornado struck about 1:00 AM when the shopping centers and school buildings were empty. Dr. Ted Fujita, tornado expert and creator of the Fujita scale to measure tornado intensity, studied the 1973 event and concluded that there were 3 distinct tornadoes that struck in the early morning hours. Why, then, were there so few fatalities in Jonesboro this time? Many speculate that after the 1968 tornado, the community was more conscious of the storms and knew what to do to protect themselves from them. Others proposed that the tornadoes skirted across roof tops and did not send their destructive winds to the ground. In the aftermath, one Jonesboro resident posted a sign in the yard of his demolished home: "Smile, God loves Jonesboro."

Chapter 6

The Deadliest and the Largest Modern Outbreaks

March 1, 1997 and January 21, 1999

March 1, 1997

A majority of tornadoes in the United States move from southwest to northeast. US Highway 67 cuts a diagonal path from southwest to northeast across the state of Arkansas (I-30 parallels this highway from Texarkana to Little Rock). Since 1950 the twenty-five counties along the US 67 corridor (including up to twenty-five miles each side of the highway) have suffered more devastation and deaths from tornadoes than the other fifty counties outside it combined. On March 1, 1997, fifteen tornadoes claimed 25 lives, injured 426, and destroyed more than $250 million in property as they followed the well-beaten path.

The Storm Prediction Center (the part of the National Weather Service responsible for issuing tornado and severe thunderstorm watches) knew that Saturday was going to be a stormy day. Warm, humid air surged northward from the Gulf of Mexico raising predicted afternoon highs in Little Rock to the mid-70s, more than 20 degrees above normal. A strong cold front was moving into the state from the northwest, dropping temperatures into the 30s and 40s. Early that morning the SPC issued a moderate risk for tornadoes for the state, and at 11:34 it issued a tornado watch for the western and central parts of Arkansas. This watch came two and one-half hours before the first tornado occurred.

Storm spotters took their positions; emergency personnel and the National Weather Service office in Little Rock went on high alert. Throughout the day NWS Little Rock issued tornado warnings for thirty-four counties (NWS Memphis issued warnings for those counties in the northeastern part of the state). Lead time, meaning the time between the issuance of the warning and the appearance of a tornado in the same area, averaged fifteen minutes. In many cases people had as much as forty-five minutes to take precautions.

The first killer tornado touched down near Hope (Hempstead County) at 1:55. During its lifetime, the twister (at places rated an F4) carved a 67-mile long path through countryside and towns before dissipating east of Malvern (Hot Spring County) 1 hour and 15 minutes later. The first fatality of this storm occurred on I-30 southwest of Arkadelphia when a forty-five-year-old man died in his vehicle that was blown off the highway.

Seeming to follow I-30, the tornado headed directly for Arkadelphia, the county seat of Clark County and the home of Henderson State University and Ouachita Baptist University. Tornado sirens blew in the town of 10,000 on a busy Saturday afternoon. At 2:42 the relatively narrow but powerful F4 twister arrived at the edge of town. As it moved through, it left everything unfortunate enough to be in its path a pile of ruins. Within minutes 30 percent of the town suffered damage, and five people perished. The injured filled the town's Baptist Medical Center; some were transferred to Hot Springs. John Overmyer, a federal emergency specialist, reported thirty business blocks and forty residential blocks sustained damages. Only one home of the fifty-seven in the Walnut Trailer Park in the southeast part of town remained intact. Two of the dead in the trailer park were teenage girls whose bodies were found on the roof of a mobile home. Two more fatalities occurred in the trailer park. Fortunately, both universities were spared. A *Dallas Morning News* article the day after the tornado gave a vivid description of the damages: "Massive oak trees that have shaded streets for decades lie scattered like so many gnawed toothpicks. Those that still stand or lean have wads of pink insulation or twisted wires hanging from their branches. Brick buildings from the turn of the century that line Main Street are missing their roofs—and occasionally a floor or two—their decorative tin ceilings slammed to the ground." Mayor Mike Kolb described his town to a *Commercial Appeal* reporter: "It's gone. It's just simply gone."

Everyone who escaped death or serious injury had a story to tell reporters from Little Rock, Memphis, and Dallas who swarmed into the town almost as soon as the winds had died down. Ralph and Beth Malone and their friend Janet Gade rode out the storm in a Toyota in the downtown area. He related that they saw the "big black cloud, but it didn't look like a tornado." Only when everything started to move and pieces of buildings scooted by did they realize what was happening. When they returned home, they found their house a total loss. Mary Faulkner said that she, her mother, her brother, and a nephew scrambled to take shelter in a walk-in closet in their double-wide home when they heard the proverbial "freight train" sound. She pulled her brother from behind a television set where the piles of debris had pinned him, but all escaped serious injury. Eric Hittenrauch, an appraiser at Horizon Mortgage Company, was in the office on Main Street with his wife and baby boy when the sirens sounded. He laid his baby on the floor in the corner of the office, and he and his wife hugged each other with the child wedged between them. Although the office lost its windows and roof, the corner where the family had taken shelter was not severely damaged; they all survived.

Every tornado leaves behind stories of odd occurrences. The entire front of a Victorian house disappeared in the storm, but a computer remained untouched on a desk. Judy Sligh wedged herself between the microwave oven and the kitchen sink in her tea shop. When she emerged, she found several items intact in the rubble--a box of glassware, a set of dishes, and her rings she had removed to wash dishes. State revenue agent Linda Miller was thankful that the storm struck on Saturday and not the previous day when more than 300 people had filled the building in an attempt to renew their car licenses. Although the tornado left only four pillars and a steel girder standing, she was able to retrieve the paper registration decals and a few new license plates from the piles of rubble; nothing else survived.

After the tornado that devastated Arkadelphia withdrew into the clouds over Hot Spring County, the parent thunderstorm produced another offspring that would bring death and destruction to Saline and Pulaski counties. This one touched down southeast of Benton (Saline County) and headed northeastward through the Shannon Hills, Vimy Ridge, and Sardis communities before entering Pulaski County. Along the way it widened to three-quarters of a mile in places and produced F4 damage. Ten died in Saline County, and five additional deaths occurred in Pulaski County; 250 sustained injuries. The hardest hit area was near Bauxite in Saline County where the twister demolished the Bennett Acres Mobile Home Park on Sardis Road; three died there. What had once been home to 60 trailers was a scene of utter devastation. Five others perished in their homes on Pine Ridge Road, and two additional fatalities occurred on Royal Oaks Drive. A short distance from Bennett Acres, the Butler Trailer Park sustained heavy damage, but no one perished. According to grocery store owner Donna White who watched the clouds from outside her store on West Sardis Road, two black clouds seemed to collide producing a tornado. She told reporters that "the wind was astronomical. It was like someone dropped an atomic bomb." Others in the area said that the funnel split in two, went around their homes, and reformed before heading northeast.

Survival tales were numerous. Leslie Gentry who had been visiting a friend at Butler Trailer Park told reporters that she didn't recognize the storm as a tornado because it was so big. The wind lifted the trailer and threw it into the nearby lake. She nearly drowned when her turtleneck got caught, but rescue workers got her out of the water nearly three hours later. Although she sustained numerous injuries, she survived. Teenager Christy Bunton was injured and her boyfriend was killed when a tree fell across the truck in which they were riding. On Pine Ridge Road, similar events unfolded. Some along the street perished while others escaped with little more than their lives. The Charles Adcock family thought they would have time to unload their groceries before the storm struck. As they hurried to finish their task, Charles glanced next door and saw a light on at the James' house and their dog tied to a pole outside. Before they knew it, the storm was upon them. The Adcocks left their groceries and ran into the bathroom, got into the tub, and covered their heads with a blanket. The tornado blew out their doors and windows and ripped off the top part of the house, but they survived. Next door at the James' the winds destroyed all of the house except the wall that divided the kitchen and bathroom. Fortunately, the family had been away visiting relatives when the twister demolished their home. A few doors away, Paul Shoemaker and his wife saw the cloud approaching and heard the roar. They jumped into the bathtub and pulled a comforter over their heads. The bathroom was the only room left untouched by the storm. Next door Danny Bowen heard the kitchen cabinets rattle then the tornado's roar. He ran to a corner bedroom for shelter; the bedroom was the only part of the home that wasn't demolished. A bedroom clock marked the time the twister had struck—3:34. Bowen's neighbor Linda Bland tried to reach her home which was up a hill behind the Bowen residence, but a tree that fell across the driveway in front of her car blocked her way. Although she thought she was going to die, she was lucky she had not been in her house. As she watched in horror, the twister destroyed her home, leaving behind bits and pieces of her life. The James' bass boat was wrapped around a tree behind what had been her house. When she began searching through the rubble, she picked up a soggy envelope. It contained a small diamond that had fallen out of her wedding ring weeks before. Charles Adcock summed up the feelings of many of his neighbors who had survived: "Some people call tornadoes an act of God. But tornadoes are just nature. The Jameses being gone, us getting into the bathroom just in time, those are act of God."

The same tornado moved into Pulaski County southeast of Mabelvale at 3:41 and traveled northeastward, damaging or destroying homes and businesses in the southern part of Little Rock. The twister partially lifted but dipped down to strike the College Station community near the airport before finally dissipating soon after it crossed the Arkansas River. Residential sections of southwest Little Rock suffered damage, but the hardest hit area was near the airport. Officials closed the facility when debris fell on runways. At the Holiday Inn-Airport winds blew out windows and peeled off part of the roof. Robert Webb, the hotel's bar and night manager, said the first indication he had that something was wrong was when the lights blinked and he felt a vibration. He and nine others lay on the floor behind the front desk. No one at the hotel was injured.

Hard hit was the College Station neighborhood just south of the Little Rock National Airport (then named Adams Field but currently Clinton National). The tight-knit black community had overcome many man-made obstacles to survive. Now this area had to deal with a natural disaster. An entire block near the community center and YMCA disappeared in the winds. Overturned cars and downed trees mixed with household furnishing and clothing, shattered windows, and sections of houses to present a heart-breaking scene. Sadly, four people in the area died. The Mount Nebo AME Church had been preparing for a youth group meeting when the storm struck. Instead, the building became a command center, and youth director Carla Halton spent the evening searching hospitals for group members.

The third deadly tornado developed ten miles northeast of Searcy (White County) and moved northeastward. Before entering Jackson County, the storm destroyed a mobile home, but the occupants escaped uninjured. The tornado grew to more than one-half mile in width and increased its ferocity to an F2 rating. Near Denmark (Jackson County) a falling tree killed two people. The tornado damaged or destroyed fifty-six homes. James Guthrie of Denmark told the *Arkansas Democrat-Gazette* that he thought he was going to die. He and his wife took shelter in their bathroom. At first he thought the sound he heard was hail, but it was the cracking of boards as his house crashed around them. Moving on to Jacksonport, the tornado continued to destroy homes and lives in its path. In the small town of 300 people, 40 homes were damaged and 13 destroyed. One man died in his demolished trailer. The wife of the pastor of the Jacksonport Baptist Church credited prayer for saving the lives of the family as well as their dog and hamster when the walls collapsed around them. The twister knocked the *Mary Woods II*, the last paddle-wheel steamboat to travel the

White River, off its mooring and destroyed the pilot house and the smokestacks. The former Jackson County courthouse, the site of a local museum, suffered a similar fate. Ducking into a vault saved museum employees from injury. The tornado continue on to Hickory Ridge where it destroyed the town's elementary school and heavily damaged several homes. In spite of the fact that the town's sirens did not sound, no one died there. The seventy-five-mile long tornado path continued on through parts of Craighead, Lawrence, and Greene counties, leaving behind minimal damage.

The day's final deadly tornado traveled twenty miles from the Marmaduke area of Greene County to southeast Clay County. At Marmaduke the twister damaged or destroyed twenty homes and killed one man at his place of business.

Several politicians had a direct connection to these tornadoes. On Sunday March 2nd President Clinton declared large parts of his home state a federal disaster area. On the Tuesday following the tornado the president said he felt "almost helpless in the face of all the destruction" he saw when he toured Arkadelphia and College Station. To him it was very personal because he recalled that as a boy he would travel by bus from Hot Springs to Hope to visit his grandparents. "I'd always stop in Arkadelphia and get a Coca-Cola and walk around the square." Federal Emergency Management Agency director James Witt, a former Yell County judge, traveled to the devastated area to see first-hand what damage the storms had done and to provide federal money for debris removal and rebuilding. Another Arkansas native, Secretary of Transportation Rodney Slater of Marianna, also toured and promised additional aid. When Arkansas Governor Mike Huckabee, a graduate of Ouachita Baptist University in Arkadelphia, saw the impacted area, he stated that "it was of apocalyptic proportions in terms of the level of destruction." He was especially sad to see that the house where he had lived while attending the university was heavily damaged. A week after the storms First Lady Hillary Clinton toured Saline County to offer words of encouragement to the area that experienced the most deaths. The mayor of the tiny Jackson County town of Campbell Station, population 247, represented the feelings of communities who had suffered damages but were ignored by the politicians and even the media. He was worried that his town that suffered great property damage but no loss of life would go unnoticed when grant money and contributions were distributed.

In spite of the death and destruction of that Saturday in March, fatalities would have been much higher if a tornado warning system were not in place. The Little Rock television meteorologists manned their radar and issued numerous warnings throughout the afternoon. The Little Rock NWS office worked tirelessly to get the information to the television stations. When the storm in southwest Little Rock knocked KATV off the air, other stations picked up the slack. KTHV used its brand new $400,000 LiveView radar, the only one in the Little Rock area, for the first time under actual severe weather conditions. Every area the tornadoes impacted had from nine to twenty-eight minutes of lead time. While warnings save lives, there is little that can be done to save property in the path of a tornado. The Arkansas Office of Emergency Services published a list of damages the March 1st storms caused. In Pulaski County 90 permanent homes, 35 mobile homes, and 10 businesses were destroyed; 175 homes and 8 businesses were damaged. In Saline County the total number of houses and mobile homes destroyed or damaged was 200. Clark County reported 45 houses and 67 mobile homes destroyed, 228 homes damaged, and more than 30 apartment units damaged or destroyed. The number of people the tornadoes impacted was much greater. Hundreds suffered injuries; saddest of all, twenty-five families suffered irreplaceable losses when family members perished.

January 21, 1999

Imagine you are a preschool teacher with the task of keeping your young charges safe when they go outside to play. Everything is fine for a while until someone notices a snake slithering onto the playground. You warn the children to stay away and hurry them toward the building where they will be safe, but before you can get everyone inside, five other snakes start slinking toward a child who has gotten free from your grasp. While you are trying to rescue this child, ten more snakes come into the play yard. You are overwhelmed by the number of slimy creatures that are trying to harm the children in your care. Now, pretend that there are fifty-six snakes threatening to harm the children. This is the predicament the NWS offices that are responsible for keeping the people of Arkansas safe from tornadoes faced on Thursday January 21, 1999. This largest number of tornadoes ever recorded on one day in Arkansas killed 8, injured 142, and terrorized 27 counties from Lafayette and Miller in the far southwest to Greene and Clay in the northeast corner of the state. The previous record was thirty-four established on June 5, 1916.

The Sunday before the outbreak several tornadoes in western Tennessee killed nine. After that day forecasters warned Arkansas that it would be its turn for severe weather late in the week—they were right! A tornado watch was in place when shortly after 3 PM the first tornado dipped from the clouds near Lerch in Lafayette County. The NWS office in Shreveport issued the first warning of the day. Before the outbreak ended after 10 PM the Jackson (MS), Memphis (TN), and Little Rock NWS offices would issue more than 100 warnings for the state (five NWS offices have jurisdiction in Arkansas; no counties under Tulsa's control were involved in the day's outbreak). As the severe weather system marched eastward, tornadoes of all descriptions formed. Some lasted only a few minutes and traveled less than a mile. Others crossed county lines during their long (by tornado standards) lives. The longest twister of the day cut a thirty-nine-mile-long path through Independence, Jackson, and Lawrence Counties. Most of the tornadoes were weak; nineteen received the rating of F0. Only one was strong enough to receive the F4 rating, but seven attained an F3 rating. Throughout the state these monsters felled thousands of trees, flattened hundreds of farm buildings, knocked down transmission towers, killed hundreds of geese, destroyed thousands of cars and several airplanes, blew apart or flipped numerous mobile homes, and damaged or demolished thousands of homes, churches, and businesses. Even one unit of the Arkansas State Penitentiary system, the Pine Bluff

Arsenal (federal government facility), and the Governor's Mansion did not escape unharmed.

White County earned the distinction of having the first deaths and the most tornadoes for the day. For three hours residents anxiously watched the sky as ten tornadoes of varying strength and length touched down across the county. Two died and two were injured near Center Hill where an F2 twister demolished several mobile homes and damaged numerous houses. More than an hour later another F2 tornado near Sunnydale claimed a life of a woman when it blew her trailer home across the line into Independence County. At Joy another storm heavily damaged the volunteer fire department. The worst White County tornado blew through Beebe about 7:30. Extensive damage occurred in both the residential and business districts as well as at the schools. The new Beebe Junior High School lost its gym and sustained other damages. The same fate awaited Beebe High School where only minutes before the storm struck a girls basketball game was in progress. The officials cancelled the game at half time and sent everyone home. Although the building suffered injuries, no people did. Paramedic Colleen McAfee was at the Beebe Fire Department when the tornado ripped the building apart. Her first concern was for her two and one-half- month old baby who was staying with her mother in the hardest-hit part of town. After navigating through fallen trees and downed power lines, Colleen reached her mother's house or what was left of it. She immediately found her mother who was critically injured but it took her over an hour to find her only child lying lifeless under a tree not far from where the house had stood.

Beebe High School gym vacated just moments before the tornado struck. NWS

A Beebe home with one wall stripped away. NWS

The most-publicized tornado of the day formed in Saline County and entered Pulaski County along Interstate 30 five miles southwest of Little Rock. The twister continued into eastern sections of the downtown area. At least 750 homes received some damage and more than 200 businesses and houses were destroyed. The MacArthur Park Historic District, Governor's Mansion Historic District, and Arkansas State Fairground neighborhood suffered the brunt of this tornado. Numerous trees crashed through fences at the Governor's Mansion. One had contained the tree house constructed for Chelsea Clinton. When President Clinton toured the storm-ravaged neighborhoods three days after they struck, he told reporters that "The fact that the Governor's Mansion, where Hillary and I raised Chelsea for 12 years, was actually in the path of the storm made it all the more real to me." He continued, "For all the tornadoes Arkansas has, and the ones that have hit around Little Rock we never had one just basically come down Main Street. We had all those wonderful old trees. It's difficult to see."

The storm also destroyed the Daisy Bates Home, a museum and national landmark in the one of the oldest areas of the city, the 100-year-old Quapaw Quarter. Daisy was one of the Little Rock Nine, and the group met at her home every morning to meet their federal escort to Little Rock Central High School and returned there after school to discuss how the day had gone. At the corner of 17th and Main the winds demolished the Harvest Foods supermarket. Derrick Stallworth who was shopping in the grocery store told reporters that the lights flickered a few times then everything went black. When he saw the roof collapsing, he hit the floor. Once the storm had passed, he helped pull some of the fifteen shoppers who had been in the store to safety. Unfortunately, Robert Howard, the store's pharmacist, did not survive. Lisa Jacko, who was driving near the supermarket, died when a tree fell on her car. Near the end of the tornado's fifteen-mile rampage James Looper died when a tree fell on his mobile home.

In spite of the unprecedented rash of tornadoes, Arkansas fared quite well. Many of the storms followed the same path as the March 1, 1997, outbreak that killed twenty-five. This time several days of preparation along with adequate warnings and a responsive citizenry kept the death toll low.

Harvest Foods Grocery in Southwest Little Rock where the pharmacist died. NWS

Chapter 7

The Longest Arkansas Tornado on Record

February 5, 2008

Super Tuesday. Americans in twenty-four states all across the country would go to the polls to cast ballots for their party's presidential candidates for the upcoming November election. Politicians hoped for a good turnout, but much would depend upon the weather's cooperation.

Six days before the tornadoes touched down and devastated hundreds of lives across four Southern states (Arkansas, Tennessee, Kentucky, and Alabama), the Storm Prediction Center (SPC) in Norman, Oklahoma, notified local National Weather Service offices in the impacted areas that they faced a high risk of severe weather on February 5. Early in the morning of that Tuesday, the SPC website's severe weather outlook map displayed a bull's eye labeled "high" over much of the state of Arkansas. As the day progressed, the weather became unusually warm for February. High temperatures reached 72° in Harrison and 74° in North Little Rock; Monday had been even warmer with both of the stations reporting 76°. In early afternoon an approaching cold front and strong jet stream combined with the high temperatures prompted the SPC to issue tornado watches for north central Arkansas. At 2:10 the SPC posted a rare "Particularly Dangerous Situation" forecast for the entire central part of Arkansas from the Missouri to the Louisiana border. The odds were great that a deadly tornado would occur somewhere within the watch area before sundown.

On the morning of February 5 storms began popping up in northeast Oklahoma, southwest Missouri, and extreme northwest Arkansas, but the conditions were not right in those areas to produce tornadoes. By midafternoon the weather in north central Arkansas felt more like late spring than winter as temperatures soared and the sun beamed down intensely. Although trees were bare, children wore shorts to school and played outside in the unusually warm weather. However, emergency management personnel throughout the region were closely monitoring the latest conditions that the National Weather Service Office in Little Rock reported. The NWS office would issue tornado warnings based upon Doppler radar or visual sightings, and the emergency managers would use their newly-established Arkansas Wireless Information Network to inform each other of potential danger in their counties.

Shortly before 5 PM the horror began when a seemingly mundane tornado touched down five miles southeast of Centerville in Yell County. Within minutes residents of Pope County received the warning that the tornado was headed their way; the storm's path would take it near Atkins. Earlier that afternoon Stacey Dollar picked up her son Devin from school and headed to check on eighty-nine-year-old Granny Estelene Boren who lived in a mobile home. Stacey took the woman home with her because of potential severe weather, situated Granny on a couch in the den, and turned on the television. Stacey paid little attention to the weather, even after her husband called to warn her that the storm was looking bad and might cross the Arkansas River. Stacey assured him that they were fine and so was the weather. Just before 5 the television lost its signal; the last thing Stacey heard on it was a warning that a tornado would be in Atkins at 5:02. Tornado sirens were sounding in Atkins. Her husband called again, this time yelling for them to get into the closet; the tornado was across the river from them and was heading their direction. Stacey managed to squeeze Devin, Granny (who needed a walker), and their two dogs into a closet in the master bedroom's bathroom; there was little room left for

Stacey. While talking to her father on her cell phone, the French doors in the master bedroom burst open and the roof began to peel back. The storm tore out exterior walls, emptied the kitchen, and hurled furniture into the front yard. Almost as quickly as it had begun, the roaring stopped. Emerging from the bathroom, Stacey saw her house was destroyed and her precious oak trees looked like match sticks, but they were safe. Several neighbors immediately rushed to help them. One antique chair remained in the house; rescuers used it to transport Granny to a truck.

Another Atkins family was not as fortunate as the Dollars were. Only a concrete slab and a few cinder blocks remained of the Cherry home where Jimmy, his wife Dana, and their ten-year-old daughter Emelaine perished. Just before the tornado struck, Dana told her mother-in-law who had called to warn of the approaching danger that they had the TV on and were looking for the storm. They were unable to reach safety in time. The terrible storm claimed the lives of two more Atkins residents before heading into Conway County.

South of Cleveland (Conway County), the monster twister killed World War II veteran Archie York and his wife Katherine when it destroyed their mobile home. Sheriff's Deputy Lamonte Chambers was on patrol when an emergency worker called to tell him that a tornado had damaged his house twenty-five miles from where he was on duty. He lived alone, so he knew that no one was injured. His path home took him through downed power lines and trees. When he got to the house, the only thing he saw standing was a hallway and the back bedroom. His home was one of thirty-three the storm destroyed in Conway County. Most tornadoes would have dissipated, but this one roared on into the next county, Van Buren.

The twister headed toward Clinton, the county seat. Sirens sounded as the threat approached the town in the growing darkness. In its path were several homes and businesses along US Highway 65, a major north-south artery in Arkansas. Residents of Lefler Estates, a three-story apartment building for the elderly and disabled, huddled on the ground floor as the tornado roared over their heads. The building's roof sustained heavy damage, but the residents were unhurt.

About 4:45 Jaclyn Derreberry of Clinton loaded her three children into her mother's car and headed south to Damascus to pick up her husband David from work. While in route, Jaclyn's mother called to warn her about possible tornadoes near Clinton. When David hopped into the car, he was hoping to get home to a hot shower and a good meal, but Jaclyn told him she did not want to be near the storms. The family headed farther south down U.S. 65 to Greenbrier where they ordered dinner and waited until the storm passed. They heard that the tornado warning for Clinton would expire at 6:15. The Derreberrys anticipated they would find the usual fallen tree branches and perhaps even some downed power lines but they did not expect what they found. At 7:15, several miles from home, they were still stuck in traffic which clogged the main highway into Clinton. David was able to take a back road to their house. After dodging downed trees and power lines, David decided to park the car and walk the rest of the way. When he got to where his house should be, he found only part of one wall standing. All of their belongings had been blown around the property when the house collapsed. David returned to the car to await the opening of the road. When they could get to where their house had once stood, the family tried to salvage what they could. David was determined to find one item, his wife's wedding ring. After searching for hours, he was successful. The house was gone, but the family was intact.

Not all families in the Clinton area were as fortunate as the Derreberrys were. Three residents perished. Sixteen men were working in the River Trail Boat factory in an attempt to finish an order that night. Just before the tornado struck, the men fled the building and took cover. Unfortunately, Thomas Armstrong was unable to get out in time. For eight hours his fellow workers dug through the piles of twisted metal and rubble trying to locate their friend. They tried calling his cell phone, but they heard no ring. Finally, they excavated Thomas's body; the coroner told them he had died instantly when the building collapsed. Most of the boats that had lined the hillside near the plant were gone. One was found fifteen miles away at Fairfield Bay. Two days later a man and woman asked the people who were working to clean up the area if they were in charge of boat removal—a boat was in her house. Rural letter carrier Tonya Selken (my husband's cousin) had chosen the site for her home carefully. Her family had observed over the sixty years they had owned the land that tornadoes seemed to skip over a dip in the ridge and touch down harmlessly on the ridge beyond. Her father remembered that once she had been in the house when a twister went right over it, but this time the Selkens weren't as fortunate. As the roaring winds approached their home, Tonya, her husband, and their two daughters huddled in the hallway. The storm lifted the trailer and threw it up the hill. All except Tonya survived. Retired merchant Fountaine Bayer died when his frame home collapsed around him. More than seventy people were injured, and sixty-four Van Buren County homes were destroyed or heavily damaged. But, the monster twister was not ready to withdraw into the clouds. It rolled across the countryside, up and down hills through forested areas, until it reached Stone County.

Directly in the path of the approaching tornado was the Stone County Medical Center in Mountain View. Hospital personnel activated their emergency response and moved patients into hallways. A maintenance worker told the administrators that he heard the roar, and it was coming down the mountain. Within seconds the tornado struck, but all seventeen patients and the staff were unhurt. Some of the hospital employees lost their homes when the twister destroyed much of the east side of Mountain View. Sadly, one resident of the area, Cathy Stodgsdill, died when the storm destroyed a friend's house where she was visiting. In Sharp County seventy-nine houses and fifty-two businesses were destroyed or damaged.

In spite of all of the lives this tornado had touched, it was not finished with northern Arkansas yet. Cattle rancher Steve Wortham lived near Melbourne in Izard County. Like many rural residents, he relied upon television and word of mouth from neighbors for warnings of approaching storms; there were no tornado sirens in much of the county. As he monitored the television which gave little information on the looming danger, he sensed something was wrong. When the power flickered off, Wortham went outside to see if it was only his house effected. As he turned to reenter his home, he heard a whistling sound and saw a tornado he estimated to be a half-mile to three-quarters of a mile wide approaching. He ran to his truck and drove across the field toward his cattle. Debris pelted the truck, but Wortham was unhurt. His cattle, though, were not as fortunate; the herd was in the direct path of the twister. In addition to losing his home, the cattleman lost much of his operation including up to 400 head of cattle, barns, and pens. His estimated financial loss approached $300,000. At the Rose Trail community in Izard County Michael Willis died when the twister blew his mobile home apart. In the Zion community a similar fate befell Jason Burkhart. At least fifty homes were destroyed and seventy more heavily damaged in Izard County.

The twister kept rolling through rural communities until it finally dissipated near Highland in Sharp County after it left behind 130 destroyed homes and businesses but no fatalities in the community. A National Weather Service survey team confirmed that the tornado had traveled a record-breaking 122 miles from 5.6 miles east-southeast of Centerville in Yell County to 3.2 miles northeast of Highland in Sharp County. Based on the extreme damage in Clinton, the NWS assigned the storm an EF4 rating with estimated wind speeds between 170 and 200 miles per hour. This was the strongest tornado to hit Arkansas since the 1997 Arkadelphia one.

Nearly everyone who survived this storm had a story to tell. At Clinton two people held onto a commode in a bathroom. After the storm, the bathroom and the commode were gone but the people were in the same place, virtually uninjured. Also in Clinton, a woman had a piece of newspaper embedded in her skin; the print could still be read. Near Zion in Izard County five people fled their mobile homes and took shelter in an egg cooling house. They chose wisely—their homes were gone but the egg house was untouched. The wife of the owner of a car dealership in Mountain View called to warn her husband that a storm was coming and wanted him to come home. Seven minutes after he left, the twister destroyed the dealership. Cars from the lot landed several hundred feet away.

Economic losses in the seven counties in the tornado's path were great. In Conway County 100 horses and more than 100,000 chickens died or had to be destroyed. Many of the chickens had been ready for market. In nearby Pope County the story was virtually the same for chickens, and in both Pope and Izard counties hundreds of cattle perished. Other businesses in the tornado's path that had employed hundreds of people counted their losses in an effort to determine whether they would even reopen. In Clinton the River Trail boat factory had employed fifty people before a direct hit left only piles of rubble and one fatality at the site. Near Lucky Landing in Pope County the owner of Bear Outdoors store estimated his losses at $800,000, more than 75 percent of his stock.

After the winds subsided, help from many places streamed into the stricken area. Under ordinary circumstances the Arkansas National Guard's 39th Infantry Brigade would be the first to respond, but these were not ordinary times. Most of the 3000-man brigade was in training at Camp Shelby, Mississippi, for its coming deployment to Iraq. Units from other guard brigades filled in for their fellow soldiers. Thirty guardsmen from Van Buren in Crawford County assisted local law enforcement officials in Atkins while security forces from the Air National Guard in Little Rock provided help at Clinton. Church groups, businesses, and individuals donated everything from clothing and food to electric generators and propane cylinders. Some sent eighteen-wheelers full of hay for livestock. One couple from Missouri who was just passing through stopped to donate baby items. By Friday a convoy from Samaritan's Purse headquartered in North Carolina brought supplies and volunteers to help with the cleanup and to offer spiritual support to those hurting from the disaster. On the Sunday after the tornado, 800 Harding University students from Searcy offered their services to the people of Clinton and Van Buren County. Some cooked meals while others repaired fences and cleared pastures of debris.

Some not in the storm's path were reminded of how ferocious Mother Nature can be. They found items belonging to storm victims who lived miles from them. One Izard County man reported that he found a receipt from a body shop located four counties away. Papers from Atkins were found in Clinton and tin was found in areas where no tin building had existed. The tornado moved whimsically and blew cars like chess pieces. Some found cars they did not own on their property while others never located their vehicles. Dwayne Guffey who lives seven miles south of Viola in Fulton County found a picture in his backyard the day after the tornado. His wife Brenda realized that it likely belonged to a family who had lost their home the day before. She made copies of the photo and sent them to newspapers in the area, hoping to locate the owner. Little did she think that a response would come from Atkins, 190 miles away. Two people in the Pope County town recognized one of the children in the photo—Emmy Cherry who had died along with her parents. Emmy's grandmother was grateful for the photo; she had located some of her son's family's belonging as far away as Timbo near Clinton, but to find a photo of her deceased granddaughter so far from the site of the destruction was incredible. In light of such stories, local newspapers posted pleas for those who found items belonging to the tornado's victims to bring them to the paper or local government offices.

A total of twelve tornadoes touched down in Arkansas on Super Tuesday, but only two were significant. Shortly before the long-track tornado dipped from the clouds miles to the south, an EF2 tornado roared through the town of Gassville in Baxter County, leaving behind 300 damaged homes, $20 million in personal property damage, and one fatality. Seventy-seven-year-old Betty Fischer died when her manufactured home in Sunny South Homes Park collapsed around her. Her husband Edmund, a Mountain Home School District bus driver who was not at home at the time, escaped injury. Most of the forty-eight mobile homes in the park were damaged or destroyed, and some residents suffered injury. Other residents of Gassville who saw the tornado approaching or heard the sirens sound escaped injury when they took shelter in various places including the hallways of their homes, the Baxter County Courthouse building, and the walk-in cooler at the Sonic Drive-in. The county's emergency management director Tom Fischer was in his car when he heard what sounded like a roaring jet and saw a house explode. He ducked under the dashboard of the car as it filled with broken windshield glass and other debris. Perhaps Krista Larcade who survived the storm huddled in her home's hallway with her three children explained the situation best. When the winds blew everything off top of the refrigerator except the Bible, she told reporters "It never budged; that's what we needed."

Chapter 8

The Deadliest Tornado That Didn't Earn a Title

Brinkley: March 8, 1909

March is a fickle month in Arkansas. Mother Nature can't decide whether it is spring or winter. In some years daffodils and jonquils bloom profusely while in other years heavy snow covers the ground. This Monday in early March was cloudy, damp, and somewhat warmer than usual; the thermometer at Little Rock registered 66° at 7 PM. In a time before radio, television, and radar citizens of eastern Arkansas had no inkling that weather systems several hundred miles to their west and southwest would impact them. Before the day ended seven tornadoes would etch this day in their state's history and leave death and destruction behind in thirteen counties.

In late afternoon several tornadoes seemingly formed at once just south and west of Little Rock. At Malvern (Hot Spring County) one tornado unroofed the courthouse and damaged several businesses and church buildings. Shortly afterward, other storms killed three northeast of Benton (Saline County) and one near Fourche just south of Little Rock. The next two hours saw five other twisters plow their way eastward across the state. One died north of England (Lonoke County), and four members of one family perished in the Zion community of Prairie County. A tornado that witnesses described as "a ball of smoke" destroyed fifteen homes and left behind three dead at Chidester (Ouachita

County). Another twister claimed the life of a baby south of Sheridan (Grant County) then killed one near Samples and another near Ferda before taking the life of a seven-year-old boy at Piney Woods (all Jefferson County). Near the same time a different tornado destroyed homes and took two lives at Witherspoon in Hot Spring County. The danger seemed over when a small twister between Staves (Cleveland County) and Brooks (Grant County) claimed no lives. Nature, however, was not finished with Arkansas. The worst tornado of the day was yet to strike.

Brinkley, located about half way between Memphis and Little Rock at the junction of three railroads, was the social and business center of Monroe County (although Clarendon is the county seat). The town of 4000 boasted good schools, two newspapers, several churches, and fine hotels to serve not only its citizens but the traveling businessmen involved in timber trade and agricultural commodities.

The day had been warm and pleasant for March. Traveling salesmen crowded the hotels, shopkeepers closed their stores for the day, and ordinary residents were finishing their evening meals when shortly before 7 PM heavy rain and a strong wind blew into the town. No news about the tornadoes that had struck to their west had reached Brinkley, so residents expressed little concern about the storm. At 7:07 the tornado blasted into town "like an explosion of dynamite", tearing a fifteen-mile long diagonal path from southwest to northeast. At times the twister, retroactively rated an F4, was more than one-half mile wide. By the time it left Brinkley, 42 residents had perished and 600 were injured. Seven additional deaths occurred in the rural areas of Monroe County. The Weather Bureau's *Monthly Weather Review* reported 260 residences and 600 buildings completely destroyed; 750 homes and 1200 other buildings received heavy damage. The business district was a total loss. The same report estimated property damage of $600,000 (approximately $1.5 billion in today's dollars). Some of the losses were the result of fires which spread through the rubble; the town's brick fire station with all of its firefighting equipment was one of the storm's casualties. Heavy rains that followed the storm brought more misery to the survivors but quenched many of the fires before they could end the lives of those buried under collapsed structures.

For a few minutes after the storm subsided the people of Brinkley, suffering shock at what had happened to them and their town, did not seem to know what to do, but before long they set about the arduous task of searching for the living and recovering the bodies of the dead. In spite of the cold rain, those who were fortunate enough to escape uninjured used the light of fires and lanterns (the city's power plant was a victim of the winds) to scour collapsed homes and businesses in hopes of finding survivors. The injured were taken to emergency hospitals set up in several places. The three Brinkley physicians labored throughout the night under trying conditions. Surgical supplies and blankets were water-soaked, but the owner of the only general store in town that survived the destruction, the Brauda Dry Goods Company, provided mattresses, cots, and other supplies to aid in care of the wounded. St. John's Catholic Church, which had escaped heavy damage, became a temporary morgue until the bodies of the dead could be sent to Helena; the Brinkley funeral homes were victims of the storm.

As soon as transportation could be found, reporters from Little Rock and Memphis newspapers rushed to the stricken town searching for survivors who were willing to tell their stories; they found enough accounts to fill their newspapers for days. In the local telephone office two operators, Lillian Coke and Edith Tabor, who took shelter in the long-distance telephone booths were unscathed when the part of the building where they usually work fell victim to the terrifying winds. They were so traumatized they did not leave their hiding place until rescuers urged them to come out. Heavy furniture saved the lives of many. Four workers at Andrew Flora's general store hid under a sturdy iron bed at the back of the building; all escaped death when the two-story building collapsed around them. Other iron bed frames saved the lives of bed-ridden Adolph Goldberg and two-year-old Robert Lee McKnight, son of one of the town's doctors. Three children of the J.C. Moshier family credited a chair and an upright piano with their survival. Others had no explanation for their escape from the tornado's wrath. Ed Livingstone explained that he, his wife, and their baby escaped injury when the entire house except the floor on which they were standing blew away into the night. Mrs. T.J. Shelby was rocking her young daughter when the winds picked up the house and threw it twenty-five feet; both were found unharmed. The congregation of the Methodist Church credited the time of the storm with their survival—one hour later the building would have been filled with revival attendees. Several families saw one family member die within their sight. Mrs. Darden and her two children were at home when the storm blew the ceiling on top of them. The mother perished, but a broken table saved the lives of the children. Reece Bunch survived in the rubble of his confectionary store but his daughter, Mrs. Ethel Phillips, was crushed to death just feet away.

Some accounts of survival were questionable. One eyewitness, Dr. O.B. Irvan, reported that he saw the winds carry a black man over 150 yards from the Rock Island Railroad tracks to the door of the pharmacy where he was standing. The man landed on his feet, seemingly unhurt but terribly frightened. Barber Bart Boyer related that the twister sucked him through a glass window in his shop and dropped him 250 feet away into a tree where he remained as the town collapsed around him.

The capricious nature of the tornado provided some relief to the survivors and filled reporters' notebooks with enough information for satisfy their readers. In the south part of town the winds picked up a child's playhouse from the porch and deposited it a half-mile away upright and unscathed; even the glass windows were unbroken. Reverend T. H. Howard found a heavy iron stove with the pipe still attached just sitting in his backyard. At a home on New Orleans Street, the winds blew the entire front of the house away but left a four-foot-high stack of crockery unbroken, although it was precariously balanced on the edge of the area where the floor was missing. In spite of the broken windows at both ends of the room and a smashed spoon holder that had once sat in the center of the dining room table, members of the E. H. Converse family could sit down for their evening meal; the remainder of the items on the table were undisturbed. The winds blew an arithmetic book three blocks and wedged it into the bell in the ruins of the city hall. Perhaps the oddest occurrence occurred at the Farrell Machinery Shop. The tornado lifted the roof from the two-story building, blew away the second story, and redeposited the intact roof on the undisturbed first floor.

People were not the only victims that night. The First Baptist, Methodist, and Presbyterian Church buildings were all piles of rubble. The city lost all of its hotels including the Arlington Hotel where seventy-five guests were spared when the tornado demolished the entire second floor. One of the local newspapers, *The Monroe County Citizen,* succumbed to the storm. The 150 employees of the Brinkley Car Works and Lumber Company lost their livelihood to the tornado's winds. The destruction of the jail, post office, and water and light plants left the town without normal services. The *Arkansas Democrat* on the following day noted that "the business section is a total loss, buildings and stock being almost worthless."

The day after the storm Governor George Donaghey along with reporters from the *Arkansas Democrat* boarded a special train from Little Rock to the devastated town. Upon arrival, the governor found himself speechless as he surveyed the utter devastation and was brought to tears when he heard of the death of a long-time friend and business associate, John H. Starrett, the state manager of the Nebraska Bridge Supply and Lumber Company. Recovering his composure, Governor Donaghey spoke to the townspeople and assured them that the resources of the state and the people of Arkansas would help them not only to survive but to rebuild. He placed the town under martial law and put the militia (National Guard) in charge of enforcing a 10 PM curfew to prevent looting. One amusing incident occurred when a guardsman ordered a well-dressed stranger who was violating the curfew to halt and produce a pass. The offender was U.S. Congressman Joe T. Robinson who had come from his home in Lonoke County to help in the cleanup. Only the intervention of the sheriff prevented the congressman from spending the night in jail. The next day the congressman volunteered to spearhead the financial relief efforts. Food, clothing, building materials, and money flooded into

Brinkley from towns and organizations throughout the state. The state coffers provided a $10,000 appropriation. Dr. E.C. Morris, president of the Negro Baptist State Convention, called upon all black churches to take up a special contribution for Brinkley on the Sunday following the tornado. Many donations came from the working class including the employees of the Rock Island Railroad and the newspaper delivery boys in Pine Bluff. Theater performances raised relief funds, and a benefit game between the St. Louis Cardinals and the Arkansaw League players netted more money for the beleaguered town. The governor sent two trainloads of prison convicts to help in the cleanup effort. It seemed as though the entire state shared in the misfortune of their fellow Arkansans.

For days after the storm blew through the thriving town on the Grand Prairie, ministers of all faiths conducted funerals. Mourners, often wearing only the clothes they had on the night of the storm, said their goodbyes to forty-nine of their own. Within days, the town began to rebuild structures and lives, torn apart by the deadly tornado of 1909.

Chapter 9

Significant Outbreaks That Did Not Earn a Title

June 1916, April 1982, April 2014

Not every deadly tornado or outbreak can earn a superlative designation, but they must be included in any history of the state's most significant severe storms. Three outbreaks meet the criteria described in the introduction although they were not the deadliest or largest.

June 5, 1916

Misinformation is abundant on the internet. Some believe that because they read it on some online website the information must be accurate. This outbreak seemed to lend itself to misinformation. Perhaps it was because local newspapers were often nonexistent at the time or were not preserved. Then, too, the Weather Bureau did not pay close attention to record keeping on tornadoes during this time period when even the mention of the word "tornado" in a weather forecast was forbidden. One glaring example of misinformation is posted on several websites—the death toll in Warren which recorded no deaths that day. The newportriweather.com site states: "June 5 1916... A tornado struck the town of Warren AR killing 83 persons. There were 125 deaths that day in a tornado outbreak across Missouri and Arkansas. (David Ludlum)." The greatest death toll from any tornado was at Warren, but the fatalities numbered fifty-five and the date was

1949 (see chapter 3). Other sites list the number of tornadoes as eighteen which is extremely low.

June is not the usual month for tornadoes in Arkansas, but 1916 was an exception. On June 5 an incredible thirty-four tornadoes (twenty-five of them significant meaning they were classified as F2 or above or caused at least one death) that touched down in twenty-five counties scattered throughout the state left behind seventy-five fatalities and hundreds of thousands of dollars in damages to structures and crops. Early in the afternoon the first deadly twister of the day claimed the life of one man near Ozark in Franklin County on the western side of the state. Marching eastward, the storm system continued to drop tornadoes in county after county; the last fatality occurred near Marion (Crittenden County) along the Mississippi River around 10 PM. Twelve counties suffered multiple deaths; seven counties recorded one death each.

The hardest hit county was Cleburne in the north central part of the state. An F4 tornado killed three people in neighboring Faulkner County before plowing through Heber Springs. Inconsistencies in reporting and duplication of names of the dead made a final death toll questionable, but the accepted number that perished in the county seat of the newly-created county (the last one to be formed in Arkansas) is eighteen, eight of whom were children. Accounts of the disaster are extremely limited. No local newspaper from the time was preserved, and no pictures were published in any paper including the Little Rock ones. The *Van Buren County Democrat* had a brief description of the tornado's path: "It struck the west part of the town extending from the school house up to what is known as 'Vinegar Hill.'" W. F. Spaunhurst recalled a few details of the storm: "There was a moment of inky blackness, a terrible roar and then timbers began to fly through the walls of the house." The Cleburne County Courthouse became a temporary hospital and morgue. Local doctors and some from other communities along with Heber Springs women worked feverishly to provide medical aid to the wounded.

On the morning after the storm the town's citizens met and decided to try to get by without outside help. They formed numerous committees to help with everything from distributing supplies to organizing funerals. Volunteers brought in wagon loads of supplies and helped recover belongings from the rubble. A businessman donated an empty storeroom and two vacant houses for those left without shelter. Local women established a soup kitchen in one room of the court house. County Judge W. T. Hammock spent much of his time responding to requests from people throughout the area who wanted to know how their loved ones had fared. The town undertaker, Thomas Olmstead, and his sons worked tirelessly, but they needed the help of volunteers to build coffins and transport bodies to the cemeteries. The day after the storms six of the town's clergymen worked together to officiate at seven funerals.

In spite of their best efforts, the citizens of Heber Springs realized that the $2800 in relief funds they had raised would not be enough to meet the community's needs. The Red Cross committee that investigated the necessities of the town determined that forty-four houses had been destroyed and eighteen others severely damaged. The town would need an additional $4000 to provide needed housing. When the two Little Rock newspapers published the Red Cross's finding, help began pouring into Heber Springs from towns and businesses throughout north central Arkansas. By the end of the week the county seat was back to work. The downtown area and businesses had been spared. The same would not be true when another tornado blew through the town ten years later (see the 1926 tornado in chapter 4).

Another hard-hit community which would suffer indescribable losses nearly four decades later was Judsonia (see chapter 2). At 5:30 PM a short, narrow F3 twister struck about four square blocks on the east side of Judsonia, killing nine, injuring thirty-five, and destroying twenty-eight homes. The wife and four children of Reverend David Pool, the pastor of the local black congregation, all perished. The church building served as a hospital for the injured black citizens, and the cotton warehouse served as a hospital for injured whites. Ed Jones, foreman of a crew laying track for the Iron Mountain Railroad, and his twenty workers were injured. The railroad sent some of their own doctors as well as a group of workers from Little Rock to help in the rescue and recovery effort. Storms struck other parts of White County, but none of these communities reported deaths or significant injuries.

Earlier in the afternoon a relatively weak (rated F2) tornado that visited Hot Springs (Garland County) followed the path of a similar twister that had hit the town only eight months earlier. Four died and twelve were injured. Property damage, estimated at $500,000, included destruction at the Oaklawn Race Track and the Majestic ball park, training quarters of the Boston American baseball team. Thirty homes, three churches, and one small business also collapsed in the storm.

Several other tornadoes claimed multiple lives on June 5th. A small, strong (F3) tornado killed seven people in three homes between Pollard and St. Francis in Clay County near the Missouri border. Five members of the William Wommac family perished near Dalark (Dallas County) when an F3 twister destroyed their home; two other children suffered injuries. Four fatalities occurred in tenant houses near Slovak in Prairie County. In Jackson County four died, including three members of one family, when an F3 tornado destroyed tenant homes near Tuckerman; reports circulated that the winds carried some bodies up to one-quarter mile. An F3 tornado hit three large farms near Forrest City (St. Francis County); four died on one of the farms. Four different tornadoes took two lives each this day. In Lonoke County a small F2 tornado killed a man and his daughter and injured twenty-two as it touched down five miles south of Cabot. At Weona Mill (Poinsett County) a tornado that blew a tree into a boarding house killed two women and injured thirteen others inside the structure. Two died on different plantations when a tornado struck south of Stuttgart (Arkansas County).

Six tornadoes (including the one in Franklin County) took one life each on that deadly Monday. Near Greenland (Washington County) one woman died when a small F2 tornado destroyed twelve tenant houses. A stronger (F3) storm killed one woman when it demolished nine homes in the Germantown community, five miles north of Morrilton in Conway County before it damaged or destroyed twenty buildings in Guy (Faulkner County). One died when a tornado cut a fifteen-mile-long path through rural Pulaski and Lonoke counties. Near Brinkley (Monroe County) one man died when an F3 tornado threw him one-half mile from his home. The last deadly tornado of the day left behind one fatality and sixty injured near Marion (Crittenden County). Six counties (Izard, Independence, Sharp, Randolph, Cross, and Lee) were fortunate enough to escape with no deaths, although tornadoes in each area destroyed homes and barns.

April 2, 1982

Note: This is one of the tornado outbreaks which has very little information available. The main source is NOAA's Storm Event Data Base.

It seemed as though deadly tornadoes had been bypassing Arkansas. The decade of the 1970s saw thirty-one deaths scattered throughout the state. The 1980s had produced only one death thus far. All would change on April 2, 1982, when fourteen tornadoes (or up to seventeen depending upon the source) struck the state leaving behind 14 dead, 92 injured, and more than $33.5 million in damages. Across the country's midsection the spring storm system produced fifty-five tornadoes and claimed twenty-seven lives, more than half of them in Arkansas.

The first tornado of the day (rated F0) touched down in Garland County in the early afternoon, damaging power lines and trees. Between 3 and 5 PM small, weak tornadoes damaged a few homes, trees, barns, and electric transmission lines in Lonoke, Prairie, and Monroe Counties. Two injuries and no deaths occurred in these twisters. Shortly after 5 PM the same parent thunderstorm produced a deadly tornado in Forrest City (St. Francis County). One person died when the twister destroyed a trailer that was being used as an office for a car dealership. Several other mobile homes, businesses, and homes as well as an elementary school sustained damage.

The deadliest tornado-producing thunderstorm of the day which took ten lives in Paris, Texas, and generated an F5 tornado in Broken Bow, Oklahoma, followed the Red River into Arkansas.

In Little River County a twister cut a fifteen-mile long path from Wallace to southeast of Ashdown. One died and two suffered injuries as this F3-rated storm damaged homes, a paper mill, and crops; one historic home built in 1834 was destroyed. As the parent storm moved into Hempstead County, it produced an F-3 tornado that meandered its way through the rural area from near McNab to east of Hope. In the outskirts of Hope a forty-foot tall tree crashed to earth in the winds crushing to death five members of one family who had taken refuge under a mattress in the center of their home. Four injuries occurred in this tornado as it damaged or destroyed forty homes.

In Sevier County another tornado this huge thunderstorm complex produced destroyed homes, mobile homes, and poultry houses as it moved slowly through Frog Level, Melrose, and Milford. After the storm crossed into Howard County, it intensified to an F4 level and took three lives at one home in the Buck Range community before lifting east of Blevins in Hempstead County. All of the southwestern Arkansas tornadoes did extensive damage to the timber industry, a major employer in the area.

Two other unconnected parts of the state endured tornado deaths that day. A very small F3 twister less than two miles in length touched down briefly near Vidette in Fulton County. Two died in one home, and two others were injured. About 7 PM, the last deaths of the day in Arkansas occurred in Conway (Faulkner County) when a strong tornado killed a nine-month pregnant young woman and her child who was stillborn. Several houses, trailers, and a machine shop sustained damage; thirty-seven were injured. Other tornadoes that touched down in Boone, Columbia, Clark, and Ashley Counties injured seven.

April 27, 2014

Residents of north central Arkansas had more than adequate notice of impending disaster. A round of thunderstorms, some producing hail, rolled through central Arkansas on the Sunday morning in April, leaving behind a distinct boundary between the cooler air to the north and west and the warmer air to the south and east. At 1:50 PM the Storm Prediction Center issued a tornado watch effective until 9 PM for most of the state. Two hours later they issued a "Particularly Dangerous Situation" (these are rarely issued) for most of central Arkansas from the Oklahoma to Tennessee border. Their main focus was the area around Little Rock. The watch included the warning that "discrete supercells moving into this environment (central Arkansas) will have the potential to produce long track….strong/violent tornadoes well into the evening." At 7:14 the Little Rock NWS office issued the first tornado warning for north central Saline, west central Pulaski, and southwestern Faulkner counties until 7:30; a tornado on the ground five miles southwest of Lake Maumelle was moving northeastward at forty-five miles per hour. At 7:29 the Little Rock NWS office sent out this message over television, radio, and weather radio stations: "Tornado emergency for Mayflower and Vilonia . . . The National Weather Service in Little Rock has issued a tornado warning for southwestern White County in Central Arkansas . . . north central Pulaski County in Central Arkansas . . . southern Faulkner County in Central Arkansas until 800 PM CDT. At 724 PM CDT. . . storm spotters and National Weather Service Doppler radar were tracking a large and extremely dangerous tornado. This tornado was located 2 miles east of Roland . . . or 5 miles northwest of Maumelle. Doppler radar showed this severe storm moving northeast at 50 mph. This is a tornado emergency for Mayflower and Vilonia. Take cover now. This includes interstate 40 between mile markers 130 and 142." (The term "tornado emergency" is used when a strong tornado with significant damage has been confirmed and is heading toward a town or city). Thousands of people were in the path of this potentially deadly storm. This section of the state was no stranger to tornadoes. Since 1953 Pulaski County had experienced eighty-three tornadoes that caused sixteen deaths. The numbers for White County were seventy-two tornadoes and nine deaths, while Faulkner County had fifty-three tornadoes and fifteen deaths.

The first area to experience the power of this forty-one-mile long monster was an area near the Saline/ Pulaski County line south of Lake Maumelle. Three members of one family died in their home near the Ferndale community. The twister crossed the eastern part of Lake Maumelle (where it turned into a waterspout) and entered Faulkner County slightly southwest of Palarm. The now EF4 intensity tornado plowed through the River Plantation subdivision and White City before striking Mayflower. The residential neighborhood of Plantation Drive suffered extensive damage. The tornado, now up to three-quarters of a mile wide, crossed Interstate 40. Unsuspecting drivers were surprised when the swirling winds tossed their vehicles about; many were thrown off the road. Heavy road construction equipment was tossed around and semis were overturned. Continuing on its path of devastation, the storm crossed part of Lake Conway and a section of Camp Robinson (a National Guard facility) then through Saltillo before leaving behind the greatest devastation at Vilonia. The monster tornado entered White County near El Paso and left behind destruction and one fatality in that county before lifting into the parent thunderstorm cloud.

Red Cross statistics revealed the devastation the tornado inflicted on a region that was no stranger to the wind storms. Faulkner County suffered most: 261 houses and 121 mobile homes were destroyed; 173 other houses and 43 other mobile homes sustained damage ranging from severe to minor. Hundreds of vehicles were mangled. Some businesses and church buildings in the storm's path were damaged or destroyed. At Vilonia the intermediate school, still under construction, was a pile of rubble. The Arkansas Game and Fish Commission removed 627 tons of debris from Lake Conway, most of which had been part of someone's life. Damage estimates were $224 million ($210 million in Faulkner County), but property can be replaced and lives cannot. In addition to the three fatalities in Pulaski County and the one fatality in White County, Faulkner County registered twelve deaths, the most in any Arkansas tornado since the 1968 Jonesboro event. In Mayflower one woman and two men died in three separate homes. The nine remaining victims were in the Vilonia area: four adult men, one adult woman, and two brothers (seven and nine years old) perished as their homes crumbled around them. One woman died in a vehicle while she was driving on US 64. An injured woman gave birth to a baby who died immediately. More than 150 suffered injuries serious enough to require hospital treatment.

As with every deadly tornado, survival stories abound. In Mayflower more than twenty people, including individuals who had pulled off I-40, crammed into Becky Naylor's storm cellar as the menacing cloud approached; all survived even though the tornado tried to rip the doors off the shelter. The George McKneelys hid in their closet as the tornado tore off the other side of their house. Mrs. McKneely's mother, a wheel-chair bound ninety-four-year-old, survived the destruction of her house without injuries. Mark Ausbrooks was staying with his elderly parents in Mayflower when he heard the tornado warnings. He related to reporters that the sky was "the weirdest color of gray I've ever seen," and that there wasn't a leaf moving. The family covered their heads with pillows as they sheltered in a closet; a huge tree fell just a few feet from them. When the storm passed, Mark looked out a hole in the house's back wall and saw I-40. He described the scene: "It looked like a kid playing with Hot Wheels, just cars everywhere and people running up and down." RVs from the dealership across the interstate from their home were scattered everywhere. Not only did Mark and his parents escape unharmed, but so did his father's rocking chair, a family heirloom. He expressed what so many in Mayflower and Vilonia felt that day: "The Lord was looking out for us, I guess."

Chapter 10

Not Record-Breakers but Important

Earliest Tornadoes, Green Forest (1927),

Center Point (1939),Berryville (1942), Pine Bluff (1947)

Not every tornado can earn the distinction of being the deadliest or the longest; yet, several tornadoes that did not meet the designated criteria are historically important. This chapter includes brief accounts of some of these.

Earliest Recorded Tornadoes in Arkansas

Tornadoes have bounced around Arkansas since its opening to settlement in 1819, but records are sparse for the early years when settlers had little time to chronicle the weather. The earliest recorded twister occurred near "the village of Little Rock" on the night of May 7, 1823. The only reported damage was the uprooting of large trees in the surrounding countryside. Another tornado that struck the same area on May 30, 1830, left behind unroofed buildings and uprooted trees. David Ludlum in *Early American Tornadoes* notes that in the overnight hours of June 6, 1840, another antebellum twister in Little Rock levelled several frame structures including the unfinished new theater. At the printing office of the *Star* the precocious winds broke the presses and scattered the type and printing materials about the building.

Green Forest: March 18, 1927

Under cover of darkness a tornado touched down four miles south of Berryville and continued northeastward for thirteen miles. In the path of the twister, at times up to a mile wide, lay Green Forest. There the storm virtually destroyed the southern half of the town and left much of the business district in shambles. An estimated $500,000 of property damage occurred. More than forty homes were completely destroyed, and more than 150 residences as well as the Green Forest School were heavily damaged. Twenty-four perished which included several entire families, and more than 100 were injured. The next morning a train from Harrison took the most seriously injured to the Eureka Springs Hospital. The National Guard, Red Cross, and Boy Scouts aided in the town's recovery. Ten years later (June 9, 1937) one died when a tornado struck the western side of town, including a canning factory and several homes that the 1927 tornado had hit.

Center Point: April 19, 1939

Four of the eight tornadoes that swarmed across southern Arkansas this day brought death. Four died in rural Jefferson County, and a woman in Miller County perished when the twister picked up her house and hurled it across the Red River. Hardest hit was Center Point, a tiny cattle-raising community near Collins in Drew County where twenty-seven died and sixty-two suffered injuries. The funeral for John Best, a farmer in the community, had just ended at the Center Point Church when the storm threatened. Most attendees rushed home, but a few took shelter in the church building. Eleven people died when a tornado, described as "black smoke boiling out of the ground" tore off the roof and one side of the building. Nine others perished on a "plantation" in the same area. Throughout the night rescue squads trudged through mud to bring out the injured and dead. The general store at Collins served as a mortuary, and the injured were treated at Monticello and Crossett.

Berryville: October 29, 1942

To the 1500 residents of one of the oldest communities in the Arkansas Ozarks the storm that approached the town about 10 PM appeared to be violent, but no one expected a tornado. Suddenly, a twisting cloud dropped from the thunderstorm and carved a half-mile wide path through the northern and western residential sections of Berryville. The houses in its path exploded. More than 600 people were left homeless. Twenty-nine died; thirteen different homes recorded at least one fatality. Rescue workers searched for survivors by torch light and candles—the winds had destroyed the town's power plant. Several businesses including the sawmill, a wholesale company headquarters, and the town railroad station were leveled. Berryville had only three doctors and no hospital. Medical help came from Harrison and Eureka Springs, and the city hall, courthouse, and Methodist Church became emergency treatment centers for the more than 100 injured. The short-lived tornado traveled only one and one-half miles before dissipating, but it left more than $500,000 damages in its wake.

Pine Bluff: June 1, 1947

Almost without exception tornadoes in Arkansas come with companions, but this was the exception. In mid-afternoon without advanced warning an F4 tornado carved a 600-yard wide path along the southern edge of Pine Bluff and into the densely-populated bayou areas outside the city. The death toll was thirty-five; incredibly twenty-one of the fatalities were children. Sixteen deaths occurred within the town including eleven black children who perished when the storm leveled a youth center. Several families suffered multiple deaths. One of the fatalities was a utility company lineman who suffered head injuries when the wind whipped copper power lines during rescue operations. The twister destroyed 50 homes and damaged 500, both in and outside Pine Bluff. Searchers combed the bayous and brakes for bodies, probing through waist-deep water strewn with the storm's wreckage. Damage estimates were $750,000.

Chapter 11

Twelve Schools and a Bridge

Although the tornadoes in this chapter's accounts did not cause numerous deaths or massive property loss, children's lives were at stake. It is the responsibility of adults, whether at school or home, to shield the young from harm. Today teachers, principals, staff members, and superintendents throughout every state are instructed on what to do to protect the students in dangerous situations, whether natural or man-made. Schools from pre-schools to universities have plans that detail what to do in the event a tornado is in their area, and communications keep leaders constantly informed of the threatening weather. Such has not always been the case. In the days before radar and weather radios, schools depended upon teacher or student observations to warn them of impending peril. Obviously, they did an outstanding job. Only twice were lives lost.

Yoder (Arkansas County): November 20, 1900

Shortly after lunch time a 300-yard wide tornado began its march across several towns in the eastern part of the state. After it killed two at Stuttgart and flattened the community of Moro, the twister headed for Yoder. The teacher at the local school loaded her fifteen pupils into a wagon in an attempt to outrun the danger; however, the storm overtook the wagon and seriously injured ten of the students. Ironically, the school building was untouched.

Lorado (Greene County): November 25, 1908

A relatively weak tornado (F2) struck a three-room school at Lorado near the end of the school day. One student died and four were injured when one end of the building collapsed.

Hoxie (Lawrence County): May 9, 1927

As the hour for school dismissal approached (3 PM), a devastating twister struck the southwest side of Hoxie and smashed into the brand new high school where it smashed the third floor and the gym; two students were instantly killed and several were injured by the falling debris. The tornado also struck the elementary school three blocks from the high school. Although the school lost its second floor, no students were seriously injured.

Rudy (Crawford County): September 29, 1927

Near Rudy an F2 tornado struck the two-story school building. Five of the 106 students in the school at the time sustained injuries when one wall of the building collapsed and students on the second floor fell into the first floor.

Village (Columbia County): December 31, 1947

At 7:30 in the evening a small F2 tornado unroofed homes and destroyed an oil derrick at Village, a community eleven miles east of Magnolia. Under ordinary circumstances, the school building would be vacant because of the holiday vacation, but this night the high school basketball team was practicing in the gym. The twister destroyed part of the gym. In the process the school's superintendent who was also the basketball coach died; none of the sixteen players were injured.

Clarksville (Johnson County): February 15, 1954

An F3 tornado that moved through Clarksville about 8 PM destroyed several homes and buildings. Among them was the gym at the College of the Ozarks. Fortunately, there were no activities at the gym; no students were injured.

Greenwood (Sebastian County): April 19, 1968

School was almost over for the week when one of the deadliest tornadoes in recent Arkansas history swooped into Greenwood. The fierce winds struck the high school. One student told reporters that the students lay down on the floor when they saw the tornado approaching. Those in a study hall hurried into a hallway just seconds before the walls of the room collapsed. No students were killed or injured at the school.

Batesville (Independence County): April 19, 1973

No tornadoes were predicted, but a ferocious F3 tornado formed over the Batesville and ripped a one-mile long trail of destruction through the town. In its path were Central Elementary School and Arkansas College (now Lyon College). At the elementary school one portable metal classroom building filled with fourth-grade students imploded. Years later one of the survivors recalled: "I felt the sensation of rising up in the air. I could see mud splashing up on the window and the dark silhouettes of people and desks tumbling through the air." In spite of the fact that only the concrete steps that led up to the classroom remained, no students were killed or seriously injured. Kathy Whittenton was a student at the college when the storm hit. She remembered that she was walking to class when she looked up to see a strange violet and yellow sky. No birds were singing; the campus was eerily silent. Professors rushed students into hallways or stairwells when out their classroom wind they saw trees bending over and rain blowing sideways. Three campus buildings were destroyed, and others were heavily damaged including the chapel, but no students were killed.

Grannis (Polk County): April 11, 1979

Shortly before lunch a powerful F3 tornado crossed into Polk County from Oklahoma. At Grannis numerous homes, trailers, and an elementary school were destroyed. Four of the thirty-five students in the building were injured as they huddled against the cafeteria wall. The school was not rebuilt.

Close Calls at Schools Not Listed Above

In spite of increased population and the use of school buildings for extracurricular activities long after the usual dismissal time, Arkansas has suffered no deaths at schools since 1927, but there have been close calls. One great fear of school administrators is that a tornado will strike as students are leaving for the day. At Belvidere, Illinois, thirteen children died, many of them on school buses that were loading in front of the high school. In Earle (Crittenden County) on May 2, 2008, school had been dismissed only twenty minutes when an EF3 tornado hit the high school. Students had been told to hurry straight home. As a result, there were no deaths or injuries at the school.

A strong tornado had been on the ground thirty minutes before it headed into Van Buren County near Bee Branch on November 11, 1988. It its path was Southside High School. The F3 twister completely destroyed the school's gym and significantly damaged other parts of the building. Fortunately, the Southside basketball team was playing an away game that night. A home game would have resulted in numerous injuries and perhaps even deaths if the usual 400 fans had packed the gym.

Tornadoes had swarmed across the state from south to north all day on January 21, 1999. In White County nine twisters had already struck several communities before the strongest one of the day, an F3, moved through Beebe at 7:25. It caused extensive damage to homes, churches, businesses, and schools. Officials cancelled a girls' basketball game at halftime, and the boys' was scheduled for a later date when word came to school officials of an approaching tornado. Fortunately, by the time the storm struck the school, the building was empty and no lives were lost.

The Edgemont Bridge

Two F4 tornadoes plowed across the northern half of the state on March 15, 1984. In their wake they left behind seven fatalities and twenty-nine injuries as well as many damaged and destroyed buildings, but that is not what made one of these tornadoes special.

At Edgemont, a community in Cleburne County on Greers Ferry Lake, the ferocious winds lifted the Highway 16 Bridge completely off its pilings and hurled it into the lake. The quarter-mile long bridge, completed in 1961, had a large steel superstructure. One Army Corps of Engineers official estimated it would have taken winds in excess of 700 miles per hour to damage the bridge in such a fashion.

The 20 Deadliest Tornadoes in U. S. History

RANK	LOCATION	DATE	DEATHS
1	Tri-State (MO, IL, IN)	March 18, 1925	695
2	Natchez, MS	May 6, 1840	317
3	St. Louis, MO	May 27, 1896	255
4	Tupelo, MS	April 5, 1936	216
5	Gainesville, GA	April 6, 1936	203
6	Woodward, OK & Higgins, TX	April 9, 1947	181
7	Joplin, MO	May 22, 2011	151
8	Amite, LA & Purvis, MS	April 24, 1908	143
9	New Richmond, WI	June 12, 1899	117
10	Flint, MI	June 8, 1953	115
11t	Waco, TX	May 11, 1953	114
11t	Goliad, TX	May 18, 1902	114
13	Omaha, NE	March 23, 1913	103
14	Mattoon, IL	May 26, 1917	101
15	Shinnston, WV	June 23, 1944	100
16	Marshfield, MO	April 18, 1880	99
17	Gainesville & Holland, GA	June 1, 1903	98
18	Poplar Bluff, MO	May 9, 1927	98
19	Snyder, OK	May 10, 1905	97
20	Natchez, MS	April 24, 1908	91

NUMBER OF ARKANSAS TORNADOES AND DEATHS BY COUNTY 1950-2020

COUNTY	TORNADOES	DEATHS
Arkansas	42	0
Ashley	40	6
Baxter	20	4
Benton	54	0
Boone	17	1
Bradley	19	7
Calhoun	17	0
Carroll	13	0
Chicot	40	1
Clark	32	6
Clay	19	2
Cleburne	28	4
Cleveland	10	0
Columbia	29	3
Conway	41	8
Craighead	42	37
Crawford	32	0
Crittenden	17	6
Cross	24	5
Dallas	25	1
Desha	25	0
Drew	19	1
Faulkner	60	27
Franklin	30	3
Fulton	20	4
Garland	31	1

Grant	26	1
Greene	32	2
Hempstead	32	5
Hot Spring	37	0
Howard	33	12
Independence	40	8
Izard	24	4
Jackson	54	5
Jefferson	32	1
Johnson	37	4
Lafayette	12	0
Lawrence	23	1
Lee	11	0
Lincoln	19	5
Little River	23	2
Logan	26	1
Lonoke	82	18
Madison	20	2
Marion	19	6
Miller	28	0
Mississippi	47	5
Monroe	20	0
Montgomery	15	0
Nevada	18	0
Newton	12	0
Ouachita	21	0
Perry	17	0
Phillips	27	0
Pike	22	0
Poinsett	36	8
Polk	35	4
Pope	25	7
Prairie	31	5
Pulaski	97	19
Randolph	15	0

Arkansas Tornadoes

Saline	52	12
Scott	8	0
Searcy	13	0
Sebastian	35	16
Sevier	19	0
Sharp	20	0
St. Francis	21	6
Stone	20	6
Union	41	3
Van Buren	34	8
Washington	35	5
White	82	60
Woodruff	35	32
Yell	30	0

Appendix C

Arkansas Tornado Deaths by Decade

This data is from Grazulis

1880's	44
1890's	93
1900's	156
1910's	158
1920's	383
1930's	103
1940's	260

This data is from the NCDC data base

1950's	123
1960's	80
1970's	31
1980's	42
1990's	51
2000's	33
2010's	40

Towns Hit by More Than One Destructive Tornado

Many tornadoes touch down in the vicinity of a town or city, but these are twisters that have impacted the town/city itself. Only those rated F2 or greater or that took a life are included.

Berryville (Carroll County)

March 4, 1939 (F2): The tornado that passed through the residential area of town injured fifteen, destroyed twenty-three homes, and damaged fifty others.

October 29, 1942 (F4): This violent tornado killed 29, injured more than 100, and destroyed 137 buildings; for additional information see chapter 10.

Bee Branch (Van Buren County)

April 29, 1909 (F2): The tornado and the fires that followed killed one, injured eighteen, and left behind $50,000 in damages; the town was described as "all but destroyed."

November 15, 1988 (F3): This strong storm killed one, injured ten, and destroyed the Southside High School gym (see chapter 11).

Camden (Ouachita County)

December 12, 1931 (F2): The twister killed one, injured seventeen, and left behind $500,000 in damages which included the courthouse that lost its upper floor.

April 8, 1979 (F3): Across the south part of town the tornado injured seventeen and did more than $13.5 million worth of damage to a school, homes and businesses.

Clarksville (Johnson County)

February 15, 1954 (F3): A very brief tornado that traveled only one mile injured twenty-four, damaged 400 structures, and destroyed sixty-eight buildings including the gym at the College of the Ozarks.

April 7, 1980 (F3): This tornado which traveled three miles through the heart of the town heavily damaged a nursing home, an elementary school, the public library, and several homes. Seventy-six were injured, most at the nursing home.

Conway (Faulkner County)

May 4, 1908 (F2): This brief "cyclone" injured eighteen and damaged forty homes and two churches on the west side of town.

May 13, 1957 (F2): One died when a brief tornado cut a narrow path through the northwest side of town. Thirteen homes were destroyed and forty-seven received damages.

April 10, 1965 (F4): On the Saturday evening before the mega Palm Sunday outbreak in the Midwest, a narrow tornado carved a path through the city's east side. Six died, and more than 100 were hospitalized.

Cotton Plant (Woodruff County)

April 6, 1909 (F2): A small twister injured one when it leveled the town's theater and several church buildings.

March 21, 1952 (F4): This tornado, one of several that formed on the deadliest day in Arkansas history (see chapter 2), decimated the northwest side of town, leaving behind twenty-nine fatalities and more than $500,000 in property damages.

England (Lonoke County)

December 24, 1932 (F2): This small tornado, only fifty yards wide, injured twelve and destroyed thirty buildings at England.

March 21, 1952 (F4): The same tornado that devastated Cotton Plant first struck the west side of England where it killed nine and destroyed forty homes (see chapter 2).

Fisher (Poinsett County)

February 23, 1909 (F4): A violent twister killed three, injured twenty-eight, and destroyed all but two of the town's thirty-nine homes.

March 15, 1984 (F4): This deadly tornado killed five and injured twelve when it obliterated eighteen homes, ten mobile homes, three businesses, the post office, and the town hall. Several other homes and businesses were heavily damaged.

Forrest City (St. Francis County)

June 6, 1974 (F3): A relatively narrow tornado (150 yards wide) cut through the western part of the town at a time shortly after 4 PM. In addition to more than 300 homes, the storm damaged school buildings and several stores in a shopping center. Four died, two at the shopping center and two in homes, and more than 100 were injured.

April 2, 1982 (F2): This tornado was part of an outbreak (see chapter 9). One died, and several businesses, trailers, homes, and a school received damage.

Fort Smith (Sebastian County)

January 11, 1898 (F4): See chapter 3 for the account of this tornado, the deadliest in state history.

April 12, 1927 (F3): See chapter 3 for the account of this tornado.

April 21, 1996 (F3): The tornado touched down on the west side of downtown Fort Smith. After causing extensive damage to a number of historic buildings in the downtown area, the tornado moved northeast through an industrial area and then into a residential area on the north side of Fort Smith. Two young children died, and forty residents of the city were injured.

Green Forest (Carroll County)

March 18, 1927 (F4): See chapter 10 for an account of this tornado that killed twenty-four.

June 9, 1937 (F3): This tornado hit virtually the same area as the one did ten years earlier. Two suffered injuries in a home where two had died in the previous tornado. Twenty-five structures, including a canning factory hit in 1927, were damaged.

Hamburg (Ashley County)

April 8, 1979 (F3): Twenty-five were injured and property losses exceeded $5 million when this twister cut a diagonal swath across the town, destroying 108 homes and damaging small businesses, schools, and a nursing home.

April 11, 1979 (F2): The odds of a tornado hitting the same town are enormous. The odds of a tornado hitting the same spot in the same week are astronomical. This second storm heavily damaged the business district, but this time there were no reported injuries.

Heber Springs (Cleburne County)

June 5, 1916 (F4): See chapter 9 for the account of this tornado.

November 25, 1926 (F4): See chapter 4 for the story of this tornado.

November 15, 1955 (F2): A small twister injured one and did more than $150,000 in damage to homes and businesses.

Hot Springs (Garland County)

November 25, 1915 (F4): A violent tornado killed ten and injured forty-five when it carved a path through the southeast side of the city. Damages to numerous homes and businesses totaled more than $300,000.

June 5, 1916 (F2): This short-lived tornado followed nearly the same path as the one of the previous year. Two hundred homes and Oaklawn Park (race track) suffered damage. One home was reportedly thrown in front of a moving train. The deaths associated with this storm were outside the city limits.

March 5, 1967 (F3): This storm injured six and damaged or destroyed eighteen homes, a gas station, and a shopping center building on the south side of the city.

Hoxie (Lawrence County)

March 20, 1913 (F2): A very brief tornado injured two and heavily damaged the downtown area.

May 9, 1927 (F4): This violent tornado tore through the town where it killed eleven including two students at the high school and injured more than 200. See chapter 4 for a more detailed account.

Jonesboro (Craighead County)

May 15, 1968 (F4): See chapter 5 for the account of this deadliest Arkansas tornado in modern history.

May 26, 1973 (F4): This twister killed one and did more than $37 million in damages. See chapter 5 for more information.

Judsonia (White County)

June 5, 1916 (F3): This tornado, part of an outbreak, killed nine and injured thirty-five. See chapter 9 for additional information.

March 21, 1952 (F4): See chapter 2 for the account of the deadliest tornado on the deadliest day in Arkansas history.

Little Rock (Pulaski County)

NOTE: Little Rock has suffered numerous tornadoes, but these are the most significant

October 2, 1894 (F3): A short-lived tornado killed four and damaged many buildings including several at the mental hospital where one doctor died when iron that fell through three floors struck him.

June 5, 1916 (F2): One of three tornadoes to strike the county this day unroofed several homes on the west side of the city.

May 14, 1923 (F2): The storm injured three, destroyed the Forest Park School, and unroofed homes in the west side of the city.

March 26, 1950 (F2): This tornado injured seven, most at a drive-in theater, then unroofed many downtown buildings before crossing into North Little Rock.

January 21, 1999 (F3): See chapter 6 for an account of this tornado which was part of the largest outbreak in Arkansas history.

Lonoke (Lonoke County)

April 17, 1978 (F2): The storm caused more than $1 million in damage and injured seven.

April 7, 1980 (F2): Similar to the above storm, this one injured one and destroyed several homes.

November 15, 1988 (F3): The price tag for this tornado that crossed the northern part of town where it destroyed several homes and businesses was $10 million.

Malvern (Hot Spring County)

March 8, 1909 (F2): One of a family of tornadoes that struck Central Arkansas unroofed the courthouse at Malvern.

December 23, 1982 (F3): One of six tornadoes this day injured twenty-nine and demolished fifty-nine homes as well as trailers and businesses. Numerous structures were damaged.

Marmaduke (Greene County)

March 1, 1997 (F3): This tornado was part of the deadliest outbreak of the modern era. One died and numerous buildings were destroyed.

April 2, 2006 (F3): A half-mile wide tornado plowed through the heart of town. Forty-nine were injured, and 130 homes were destroyed. Heaviest damage was done to the American Railcar Industries plant.

Mena (Polk County)

November 23, 1908 (F2): Two died in a tornado that swept across the northern part of town.

April 13, 1911 (F2): This narrow tornado (100 yards wide) injured two and unroofed numerous buildings in a fifteen-block area of downtown.

November 13, 1993 (F2): The storm destroyed or heavily damaged homes in the southwest section of town. Eleven were injured. Large trees at the city park, some more than 100 years old, were casualties.

April 9, 2009 (EF3): Three died and thirty were injured when a wide, violent tornado tracked through the city. More than 700 homes, numerous businesses, a nursing home, the Polk County Courthouse, the county jail, Mena City Hall, and the police and fire department were damaged. Mena Middle School and 165 homes were destroyed.

Pine Bluff (Jefferson County)

August 15, 1883 (F1): One woman died when a post in front of a store fell on her as a very weak tornado passed through Pine Bluff at roof-top level.

May 11, 1910 (F2): A miniscule tornado (path length was only one-half mile long and fifty yards wide) injured five and damaged several homes on the southeast side of town.

June 1, 1947 (F4): See chapter 10 for the account of this tornado.

Vilonia and Mayflower (Faulkner County)

April 25, 2011 (F2): An extremely wide tornado (nearly one and one-half miles at times) killed four and heavily damaged homes and businesses in both towns.

April 27, 2014 (F4): This devastating tornado destroyed homes and killed nine in Vilonia and three in Mayflower. See chapter 9 for the account.

Warren (Bradley County)

January 3, 1949 (F4): See chapter 3 for the account of this deadliest tornado in Arkansas history.

March 28, 1975 (F4): See the end of chapter 3 for this tornado's story.

Sources

Newspapers

Arkansas Democrat
Arkansas Democrat-Gazette
Arkansas Gazette
The Baxter Bulletin (Mountain Home)
Commercial Appeal (Memphis)
Dallas Morning News
The Eagle Democrat (Warren)
Fort Smith News
Greenwood Democrat
Jonesboro Sun
Northwest Arkansas Times (Fayetteville)
Salt Lake City Semi-Weekly Tribune
Southwest Times Record (Ft. Smith)
Van Buren County Democrat (Clinton)

Books and Articles

American Meteorological Society. *Monthly Weather Review*. Boston, MA. Various dates.

Arkansas State Highway Commission. "Damaged Bridge Being Replaced." *Arkansas Highways* 30 (Summer 1984): 12.

Ashley, W. S. "Spatial and temporal analysis of tornado fatalities in the United States: 1880-2005." *Weather and Forecasting* 22 (2007): 1214-1228.

Bradford, Marlene. *Scanning the Skies: The History of Tornado Forecasting.* Norman: University of Oklahoma Press, 2001.

Burkett, Lucille Tucker. "The Story of a 1929 Tornado and Its Effect on a Woodruff County Family." *Rivers and Roads and Points in Between: Woodruff County Historical Society Journal* 12 (Fall 1984), pp. 23-28.

Grazulis, Thomas. *Significant Tornadoes 1680-1991.* St. Johnsbury, VT: Environmental Films, 1993.

Hanley, Ray. "Death Wind Blows across the Grand Prairie of Arkansas." *Central Delta Historical Journal* 1 (Feb. 1997): 10-19.

Ludlum, David. *Early American Tornadoes, 1586-1870.* Boston: American Meteorological Society, 1970.

Orr, W. E. *That's Judsonia.* Judsonia, AR: White County Printing Co., 1957.

Porterfield, Jan. "1926 Tornado." *Cleburne County Historical Journal* 30 (Winter 2004): 123-141.

Porterfield, Jan. "Cleburne County Tornadoes." *Cleburne County Historical Journal* 30 (Summer 2004): 62-80.

Government Documents and Websites

National Aeronautics and Space Administration. "Environmental Statement for Applications Technology Satellite Program." Washington, D.C.: 1971.

Sources

National Climatic Data Center Storm Events Database. http://www.ncdc.noaa.gov/stormevents/

National Weather Service Forecast Office, Little Rock, AR. "Severe Weather on February 5, 2008." http://www.srh.noaagov/lzk/?n=svr0208yr.htm

National Weather Service Tornado Database. http://midsouthtornadoes.msstate.edu/index.html

Tulsa Tornado Tribune: www.srh.noaa.gov/meia/tsa/tribune/Spring2013.pdf

U. S. Department of Commerce, National Oceanic and Atmospheric Administration, National Weather Service. *March 1, 1997, Arkansas Tornado Outbreak: Service Assessment.* Silver Spring, MD: 1997.

U.S. Department of Commerce, National Oceanic and Atmospheric Administration, National Weather Service. *Super Tuesday Tornado Outbreak of February 5-6, 2008: Service Assessment.* Silver Spring, MD: 2009.

Other Websites

A Tale of Two Towns, http://ataleoftwotowns.com/1927-hoxie-walnut-ridge-tornado/

Gendisasters. www3.gendisasters.com/arkansas

Incredible Stories of Tornado Survival in Arkansas, Kansas http://www.weather.com/news/news/survivors-recall-escaping-deadly-tornadoes-arkansas-kansas-20140428

Lyon College. https://www.lyon.edu/news/tornado-cross-provides-campus-symbol-rebirth-hope

Old State House Museum, Arkansas News, "Tornado Warning in Strong Starts Sad Day in May." http://www.oldstatehouse.com/collections/classroom/arkansas_news.aspx?issue=32&page=8&detail=458

One Hundred Fifty Years of Sebastian County. http://www.sebastiancountyar.gov/Portals/0/Content/Misc/150%20Years%20of%20SebCo.pdf

James Skipper's Judsonia Tornado Page. http://jamesmskipper.tripod.com/jamesmskipper/tornado.html

"Tornado Survivor in Mayflower, Ark., Describes Terror," http://www.nbcews.com/storyline/deadly-tornado-outbreak/tornado-survivor-mayflower-ark-describes-terror-n9

The Weather Channel "Mayflower, Vilonia, Arkansas, Tornado: Timing of National Weather Service Warnings Undoubtedly Saved Lives,"http://www.weather.com/news/news/mayflower-vilonia-tornado-nws-warnings-save-lives-20140428

Mike Wilhelm's Alabama Weather Blog Bamawx.com: Two PDS Watches. http://www.bamawxcom/2008/02/two-pds-watches.html

About the Author

Marlene Bradford has spent most of her life in Tornado Alley. When living in Lawrence, Kansas, Joe Eagleman, a meteorology professor at the University of Kansas, encouraged her to write tornado history. Her doctoral dissertation at Texas A&M University was the story of the tornado watch and warning system which was published in 2001 by the University of Oklahoma Press under the title *Scanning the Skies: A History of Tornado Forecasting*. She is also the author of *Texas Tornadoes: The Lone Star State's Deadliest Twisters* and the editor of *Notable Natural Disasters*. Her love (besides tornadoes) is teaching. The author has recently retired from more than twenty years of teaching U.S. history at the college and high school level and currently resides with her husband in Garland, Texas.

www.ingramcontent.com/pod-product-compliance
Lightning Source LLC
Chambersburg PA
CBHW072142280526
45788CB00002B/755